Exploring tough questions facing youth today

MANTRAS, MENORAHS, AND MINARETS

Encountering Other Faiths

ISBN 978-1-949628-16-6
Printed in the United States of America.
10 9 8 7 6 5 4 3 2 1   22 21 20 19

Published by The Pastoral Center, http://pastoral.center.

Developed in partnership with MennoMedia and Brethren Press. Series editors: Fumiaki Tosu, Ann Naffziger, and Paul Canavese. *Mantras, Menorahs, and Minarets:* Writer, Gary Wilde. Project editor, Lani Wright. Staff editors, Susan E. Janzen, Julie Garber, and James Deaton. Updated design, Paul Stocksdale.

All rights reserved. Purchase of this book includes a license to reproduce this resource for use in a single parish, school, or other similar organization. You are allowed to share and make unlimited copies only for use within the organization that licensed it. If you serve more than one organization, each should purchase its own license. You may not post this document to any web site without explicit permission to do so. Outside of these conditions, no part of this book may be reproduced in any form or by any means, electronic or mechanical, including photocopying, recording, taping, or via any retrieval system, without the written permission of The Pastoral Center, 1212 Versailles Ave., Alameda, CA 94501. Thank you for cooperating with our honor system regarding our licenses.

For questions or to order additional copies or licenses, please call 1-844-727-8672 or visit http://pastoral.center.

Portions of this work © 2019 by The Pastoral Center / PastoralCenter.com. Adapted and published with permission from Generation Why Bible Studies. © 1997, 2015 Brethren Press, Elgin, IL 60120 and MennoMedia, Harrisonburg, VA 22803, U.S.A. All rights reserved.

Unless otherwise noted, the Scripture passages contained herein are from the *New Revised Standard Version of the Bible*, copyright © 1989 by the National Council of the Churches of Christ in the United States of America. Used by permission. All rights reserved.

>> OVERVIEW

When conversing online, the acronym IRL stands for "in real life." The virtual world of social media, text chats, blogs, and more have the power to remove us from the real world. What we experience online can skew our perspective on what it means to be human. It can numb us, incite us, distract us, depress us, confuse us, and make us rude or impatient. Strangely, this supposedly "social" and "connected" technology can profoundly disconnect us from others.

Religious faith can also place us in a bubble, especially when it distances us from others. When we keep the prophetic message at a safe distance, obscured in theological language and abstractions, we are missing the whole point. And when we see our parish as an insider club that serves itself, we can forget the radically inclusive message entrusted to us: God's love is for *everyone*, and God expects us to transform the *whole world* through that love.

Through the incarnation, God showed up in the real world to show us that our faith is not just about talking the talk, but also walking the walk. It can be risky. It can be confusing. It can hurt. But living out our faith can also bring us great purpose, peace, and joy.

This series connects the Bible with the tough questions that youth (and adults) encounter in their neighborhood, in school, among friends, and even online. This process will help you as a leader break open these issues in a fun and meaningful way, sparking conversation and the kind of life change Jesus invites us to embrace.

>> THE ROLE OF PARENTS

As children enter middle school and high school, they become more independent, self-reliant, and, well, self-centered. This can bring parents to make assumptions that this is the time to step back, giving their child more space to form their identity. While there is truth to that at some level (adolescents definitely shouldn't be smothered), this is a stage of life when parents should in fact *lean in*. The apparent confidence and bluster youth show on the outside can mask the insecurity and confusion on the inside. Youth need their parents to be involved more than ever.

>> WHOLE FAMILY FORMATION

Parents are the primary teachers of their own children, and parishes are waking up to the fact that faith formation programs need to bring parents into the process if they hope to see faith passed on to the next generation. Recent studies give us more and more evidence that the role of parents is the most important factor in determining whether a child will embrace faith as they move toward adulthood. Research from the Center for the Applied Research on the Apostolate shows that parents who talk about their faith and show through their actions that their faith is important to them are more likely to have children who remain Catholic.

More about Whole Family Formation >>>>

To learn more about how your parish can take a comprehensive whole family approach to faith formation, visit **GrowingUpCatholic.com**.

While whole family events with elementary-aged children are on the rise, the role of parents can be an afterthought in youth ministry. We have designed the sessions in this series to work with or without parents present, and we encourage you to offer them as parent-child events.

If you choose to involve parents, it is important to consider before each session how to best do so. Many of the activities in this series are high-energy, creative, or silly. Some parents may need some encouragement to get out of their heads and have fun with the group. A few activities involving physical contact would be inappropriate for parents and youth to participate together, and we have noted them as such.

There are a number of ways to approach discussions with parent participation. Unless you have a small group, you will likely want to break into smaller groups for conversation. Some youth may be self-conscious and unable to be completely honest and open in a group situation with a parent present. For this reason, you may choose in some cases to assign parents to different groups from their own children, or to have separate parent and child groups altogether. Be sure to cover expectations around confidentiality. It is inappropriate for a parent (or youth) to share with another parent what their child said in a small group.

Note that even if parents and their children do not share all conversations together in the session, they will still have a valuable shared experience and can have extended conversations about it later.

>> THANK YOU

The role you play in gathering, animating, praying with, and forming youth is a valuable one. Thank you for all you do to serve the church and its families!

Bible-based Explorations of Issues Facing Youth

MANTRAS, MENORAHS, AND MINARETS
Encountering Other Faiths

>> INTRODUCTION

"What is truth?" It's an age-old question, that's what it is. God is bigger than anything we can think about God. Therefore, we can learn from others' thoughts and beliefs—and from their unfamiliar theologies. We can expand our truth-horizons!

Our Catholic tradition encourages us to engage in this kind of dialogue. At the Second Vatican Council, the bishops themselves expressed a desire to enter into conversation with the entire human family, including followers of other faiths (*Pastoral Constitution on the Church in the Modern World*, 3, 92). In a separate document, the *Declaration on the Relation of the Church to Non-Christian Religions*, the Council Fathers urged us to enter the dialogue in order to "recognize, preserve and promote the good things, spiritual and moral, as well as the socio-cultural values found among" the followers of other religions (*Declaration on the Relation of the Church to Non-Christian Religions*, 2).

The Church's attitude toward other religions is one of deep respect and reverence:

> The Catholic Church rejects nothing that is true and holy in these religions. She regards with sincere reverence those ways of conduct and of life, those precepts and teachings which, though differing in many aspects from the ones she holds and sets forth, nonetheless often reflect a ray of that Truth which enlightens all people. (*Declaration on the Relation of the Church to Non-Christian Religions*, 2)

Being human comes with basic questions about the purpose and problems of living, and religion is the way humans have wrestled with the fundamental issues of life. So how do the basics of the Christian religion compare and contrast with other major religions? This encounter with other faiths will follow this basic outline:

Session 1 (The Religions): The "God Question" *encounters* revelation.
Session 2 (Hinduism): Karma *encounters* grace.
Session 3 (Buddhism): "Suffering escaped" *encounters* "suffering transformed."
Session 4 (Judaism): Christianity *encounters* its roots.
Session 5 (Islam): Absolute certainty *encounters* a growing faith.

Preparation Alert >>>>

Make preliminary plans (or set up a committee) to:

- **Visit sites** of other religions and their worship; and/or

- **Invite** adherents of these faiths to give their personal testimonies to your group, or lead the group in a prayer experience from their tradition.

> "[S]ome might ask: why does the Pope go to the Muslims and not just to Catholics? Why are there so many religions... [God] willed to permit this reality: there are so many religions; some are born of the culture, but always looking to heaven, looking at God. However, what God wills is fraternity among us in a special way... We must not be scared by the difference: God has permitted this...To serve hope, at a time like ours, means first of all to build bridges between the civilizations."
>
> Pope Francis
> Visit to Morocco
> April 3, 2019

In these sessions, do not come expecting to *understand* the religions, or to debate them. They cannot be fully explained or described in a short course like this. However, you can get a feel for them and their basic point of view. This will happen with even more impact and immediate relevance if you'll do three things. Make every effort to:

(1) **Visit sites** of other religions and their worship; and/or

(2) **Invite** adherents of these faiths to give their personal testimonies to your group. Prepare for such interactions by developing a set of questions in advance for each visit/visitor. For example:

- *How did your religion begin? Is there one founder? What is his or her story?*
- *Do you worship a god? What is your belief about God?*
- *In your religion, what is considered the basic question/problem about life? How is a person "saved" from this problem?*
- *How has knowledge of truth come to you/your religion? What is the nature of revelation?*
- *What is your view of Jesus?*
- *What rules must your adherents follow?*
- *How does your religion view the concepts of love and grace?*

(3) Ask leaders of other faith traditions to lead the group in an experience of a **ritual** or **prayer** central to that belief system.

You'll no doubt deal with other tough questions at some point during your course. Examples include: "Is Jesus really the only way?" and "Why should I commit to Jesus when other religions also claim to have truth?" and "Can I respect another person's beliefs and still invite them to become Catholic?"

Ultimately, such questions can only be answered by each individual truth-seeker over an entire lifetime. But you might offer these directions for discussion:

1. **Why Jesus?** When people have wholeheartedly committed to Christianity, they have discovered a **uniqueness** about Jesus compared to the gods of other religions. The most unique aspect is the claim of resurrection. (The exploits of Arjuna and Krishna in the *Bhagavad Gita* have a historical backdrop, but are not considered to have actually happened in space/time.) In gathering the evidence for it, such people also claim a personal experience: the indwelling presence of Jesus, being inspired by holy writings, warmed by fellowship, called and influenced by the Spirit. But all these claims must be wholeheartedly checked out by any individual seeker wanting to know the truth.

2. ***Can I respect another person's beliefs and still invite them to convert to Christianity?*** Remember three things:

    - *We are called to witness, but only God can convert.* Do you believe that God has called you and saved you? If so, you can let God do the calling of others, just as God has called you.
    - *Our witness is a confession of both personal knowledge and recognition of ignorance.* We may believe that reality is a certain way, but we must be willing to have our beliefs put to the test, as well as recognize aspects of truth in others' beliefs, too.
    - *We are all in the process of either moving closer or further from the truth,* each moment. C. S. Lewis put it this way: "There are people who are slowly ceasing to be Christians but who still call themselves by that name.... There are people in other religions who are being led by God's secret influence to concentrate on those parts of their religion which are in agreement with Christianity, and who thus belong to Christ without knowing it." (*Mere Christianity*)

When we encounter other religions, our first duty is not to convert, but, as the bishops say, to "recognize, preserve, and promote the good things" —and there are many!—found in other religions.

One other thing: A course like this requires a bit more information-giving than most other topics for youth. That's why there's a handout sheet for every session of this unit. In addition, experiencing a ritual central to each of the religions, either during a visit to a worship site or during your sessions under the leadership of an appropriate faith leader, will help elicit questions and expand horizons.

You'll want to dig even deeper into the religions before you face your group's tough questions. Become informed by committing to a personal study program—work with the Internet, visit your local library, and have on hand at least one good text on each of the religions you'll be studying. Read out of the appropriate text before each session. You'll be better informed, feel more confident, and exude a deeper enthusiasm as you lead the group. Studying the religions is truly an exciting exploration!

Recommended books:

- Eliade, Mircea. *The Sacred and the Profane* (New York: Harcourt, Brace & World, Inc., 1959). A classic on the philosophy of religion.
- Evans, C. Steven. *Philosophy of Religion* (Downers Grove IL: InterVarsity Press, 1985).
- Fitzgerald, Michael and John Borelli. *Interfaith Dialogue: A Catholic View* (Maryknoll NY: Orbis Books, 2006)). https://pastoral.center/interfaith-dialogue
- Kasper, Cardinal Walter. *Towards Unity: Ecumenical Dialogue 500 Years after the Reformation* (Mahwah NJ: Paulist Press, 2017). https://pastoral.center/towards-unity
- Neill, Stephen. *Christian Faith and Other Faiths* (Downers Grove IL: Intervarsity Press, 1984). An Evangelical perspective on the religions.
- Shenk, David. *Christian, Muslim, Friend: Twelve Paths to Real Relationship*. https://pastoral.center/christian-muslim-friend
- Smith, Huston. *The Illustrated World's Religions: A Guide to Our Wisdom Traditions* (San Francisco: HarperCollins). "…Considered to be the most eloquent and accessible introduction to the world's religions available." https://pastoral.center/the-illustrated-worlds-religions
- Thich Nhat Hanh. *Living Buddha, Living Christ* (Riverhead Books, 1995). "Drawing on many years of interfaith exchanges begun during his peace trips to America, Nhat Hanh…offers bridging insights into points where Buddhist and Christian practices meet. In so doing, he encourages Westerners to see the 'jewels in their own tradition' with fresh eyes." Also by Thich Nhat Hanh: *The Miracle of Mindfulness*.
- More resources can be found at https://pastoral.center/religion.

Videos and websites:

- A "tour of religions" is found at http://www.bbc.co.uk/religion/religions/.
- Tabs on the website Beliefnet (BeliefNet.com) offer information and prayers from major religions.
- http://ed.ted.com/lessons/the-five-major-world-religions-john-bellaimey. This is an 11-minute TED Talk overview of each of the world's five major religions. Summarizes the main points you are teaching, with the addition of maps, and ties the facts of each religion together very nicely.
- https://youtube.com/playlist?list=PLVIONUaVP3zLdtRt6SebKQhevqGkZcPSd. Religions of the World Series, narrated by Ben Kingsley, available on YouTube.
- https://www.flocabulary.com/major-world-religions/. Includes songs, video, challenge questions, and a teacher's guide, but also requires signing up for a free trial in order to use the resources.

"…All of us of every faith tradition possess the possibility of pure light, is that not so? The question of who we are is very much open."

His Holiness the Dalai Lama

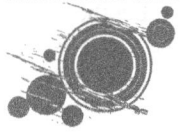

Nostra Aetate

The full text of the document *Declaration on the Relation of the Church to Non-Christian Religions* can be found here:

http://www.vatican.va/archive/hist_councils/ii_vatican_council/documents/vat-ii_decl_19651028_nostra-aetate_en.html

EXTENDER SESSION

Extender sessions suggest special activities related to the issue of the unit. They help accommodate the diversity of parish schedules. Since each unit is undated, participants may study units in their entirety and still participate in special events of the parish that get scheduled simultaneously with youth group time. Extender sessions can be used anytime, but the one for this unit best follows **Session 5**. Calculate now whether or not you will be using the extender session.

- Karen Armstrong's *A History of God* can be viewed as a full-length documentary at http://topdocumentaryfilms.com/a-history-of-god/. Based on her best-selling book, the video traces the evolution and interrelation of the various Christian, Jewish, and Islamic interpretations of the divine figure. Through balanced analysis of historic and holy texts and extensive use of ancient art and artifacts, it follows the long road to today's understanding of God and what the journey—and the destination—have to tell us about humanity and its never-ending search for meaning and comfort.

THE SESSION PLAN: The parts of the session guide

» **Faith story.** The session is rooted in this Bible passage and compared with a basic story of another religious faith.

» **Faith focus.** The comparison/contrast in a nutshell.

» **Session goal.** The entire session is built around this goal. What changes—in knowledge, attitude, and/or action—do you desire in your group?

» **Materials needed and advance preparation.** This is what you will need if the session is to go smoothly. You'll feel more at ease if you've taken care of these details before you meet your group.

» FROM LIFE TO BIBLE TO LIFE

The teaching plan is called *life-centered*. However, when we write each session, we always begin with the faith stories.

In every session we try to hit upon a tough question that youth might ask. Find out what questions on this issue are important for your group. Feel free to bring your own input and invite your group members to add their own experiences.

» TEACHING THE SESSION

The five step-by-step movements will carry you from *life to the faith stories and back to life*. Each session takes about 45 to 50 minutes. Using the handout sheet for the session, take note of any complementary activities and stories.

1. **Focus.** Intended to create a friendly climate within the group and to *draw attention* to the issue.

2. **Connect.** Invites participants to *express* their own life experience about the issue, through talking, drawing, role playing, and other activities. Also uses memory, reason, or imagination to get the group thinking about *why* they view the issue the way they do.

3. **Explore the Stories.** With a minimum of lecturing, dig into the faith stories and search for answers to questions raised in the first activities. The Insights section will help clarify.

4. **Apply.** What do the stories *mean* for contemporary life? This is the "aha!" moment when participants realize the faith story has wisdom for *their* lives.

5. **Respond.** Why do the faith stories *matter*? What will the group do about the issue in light of what they have learned from their own experiences set alongside the faith issues? How can we *live* faith rather than pass it off as a mere intellectual exercise?

» LOOK AHEAD

Here are reminders for what you need to do for the next session or two.

» INSIGHTS FROM HOLY WRITINGS

Here is a resource for Explore the Stories. Don't try to use all the material given. Take what you need to lead the session and answer questions your group may have. Let the Insights section inspire you to think and study more about the focus of the session.

» HANDOUT SHEETS

The writer has provided a handout sheet to complement each session. Make enough copies for the group in advance of the session. These sheets may include questions, stories, agree/disagree exercises, charts, pictures, and other materials to stimulate thinking and discussion.

Generally, no participant preparation is required unless the session plan calls for you to contact selected group members for specific tasks.

SESSION 1

WHICH WAY TO GOD?

KEY VERSE

"For as I went through the city and looked carefully at the objects of your worship, I found among them an altar with the inscription, 'To an unknown god.' What therefore you worship as unknown, this I proclaim to you." (Acts 17:23)

FAITH STORY

Acts 17:16-34

FAITH FOCUS

The apostle Paul went to Athens to "reason with" those he found in the local synagogue and in the marketplace. When certain philosophers questioned him about his teachings, Paul was ready with answers. In gaining a hearing, he started where his hearers were, referring to their worship of an unknown god. With his usual logical precision, Paul attempted to persuade them that the God they called "unknown" was in truth the Creator of all—the One who had already risen from the dead.

Some in the audience wanted to know more. For others, however, talk of a resurrection was too much. They sneered and turned away.

SESSION GOAL

Help participants identify some of the questions humans ask about ultimate meaning, so they can consider how to relate to people of other religions.

TEACHING PLAN

» Materials needed and advance preparation

- In advance, write (on a chalkboard or newsprint) a basic outline to guide the group in creating a "perfect" religion (Focus, *Option A*).

- Copies of a quotation (Focus, *Option B*)

- Bibles

- Copies of the handout sheet for Session 1

- Large sheet of newsprint with a question mark drawn in the center (see Apply), markers and/or crayons, tape

- Gather editions of the religion section from your local newspaper, along with one or more local phone books (see Respond). *Option*: Access these via the Internet and social media connections.

1. FOCUS 10-12 minutes

» **Option A: Create-a-religion.** When everyone has gathered, present this scenario:

Imagine: This group has suddenly been carried off by a band of aliens from outer space! You land on a faraway planet. You ask, "What do you want with us?" Comes the response: "We want a religion. We will not let you leave until you develop the perfect religion for us." As you look around, you realize that the inhabitants of this planet are human beings exactly like you! You must decide: What will be the perfect religion for these people?

In Real Life | Mantras, Menorahs, and Minarets 11

> "People expect from the various religions answers to the unsolved riddles of the human condition... What is the meaning, the aim of our life? What is moral good, what is sin? Whence suffering and what purpose does it serve? Which is the road to true happiness? ...What, finally, is that ultimate inexpressible mystery which encompasses our existence: whence do we come, and where are we going?"
>
> *Declaration on the Relation of the Church to Non-Christian Religions*, 1.

Unveil, on the chalkboard or newsprint, a basic outline to guide thinking:

- What needs will this religion have to meet?
- What questions about life will it try to answer?
- Name of the religion:
- Key belief of this religion:
- Description of deity (if you choose to have one):
- Key benefits to worshipers (What are they? How do we get them?):
- Rules (if needed):
- How would people be able to tell if you were a member?

Let participants know that using humor is okay, but stress that they should try to make their religion "perfect" by *first determining what human needs it would have to meet and what questions it would have to answer*. They should try to make it very practical—a religion that would meet young peoples' needs and questions, a faith they would want to join.

When the group has had a chance to work at this, gather everyone together and report results. Then discuss: *What needs does a religion have to meet? In your opinion, are these needs common to all humans? Explain.*

Option B: Open with a simple quote-reaction exercise. Copy the James Fowler quote from the book *Stages of Faith*, so that everyone has a few moments to study it:

> **Faith is a universal human concern. ... Before we come to think of ourselves as Catholics, Protestants, Jews, or Muslims, we are already engaged with issues of faith. Whether we become non-believers, agnostics, or atheists, we are concerned with how to put our lives together and with what will make life worth living. Moreover, we look for something to love that loves us, something to value that gives us value, something to honor and respect that has the power to sustain our being.**

Then ask:

- *What is Fowler trying to say? What does it mean? What does it mean for you and any questions you have about what "religion" is?*

2. CONNECT 5 minutes

Invite participants to define religion as it comes closest to their own *present understanding*: "Religion is...". Ask them to give reasons for their definitions. After brief sharing, offer this suggestion (write it on the chalkboard or make a poster of it) as a basic definition that could be used throughout this course:

> **Religion is the expression of and response to that which people hold as being of unrestricted value for them.**

Ask:

- *What is of unrestricted value for you? What is so true for you that it seems self-evident? What value surpasses all other values? What commands and receives your best time and energy?*
- *In light of our definition, is everyone religious? Explain.*

3. EXPLORE THE STORIES 12-15 minutes

Shift to this activity by saying: *In digging into religion, we are dealing with the deepest human needs and longings—for love, acceptance, security, and meaning in the face of suffering and death. It's also about trying to make sense of life's most profound questions. In the Bible, when the apostle Paul visited some worshipers, he encountered such longings and questions....*

Pass out Bibles and invite participants to turn to Acts 17 and follow along as you read aloud verses 16-34. Then ask:

- *What do you think Paul meant when he said: "I see that in every way you are very religious"?*
- *What questions about life's needs and meaning were the worshipers apparently asking? What answers did Paul offer?*
- *How do these needs and questions compare to those people might express today?*
- *Describe, in your own words, what Paul was saying to these people.*

Now distribute copies of the handout sheet and divide into three groups, one for each of the three "Big Questions." Explain that these are often the first questions many people ask when they start to think about Christianity and its relationship to other world religions. Say something like: *Dealing with these questions up front will help us set the stage to study specific religions.* Let participants know that in a moment they'll have a chance to raise other questions.

The task is simply to choose one or more of the entries under "Possible Insights" to link with their assigned Big Question. They are to discuss the question and be ready to share how the Insight entries might lead to a potential answer for them.

Leave this discussion time as open-ended as you wish. When groups report, supplement, if necessary, with your own explanations, drawing from the Insights section.

4. APPLY 10-12 minutes

Ask:

- *How satisfying are your answers to such questions so far? What questions still remain in your mind?*

Unroll a large piece of newsprint with the huge question mark drawn in the center, and invite participants to jot "More Questions We Want to Answer" on this paper. Give everyone a marker and begin brainstorming and writing, neatly enough so that the paper can be hung on a wall and left there for all five sessions of the unit. (You'll be able to check periodically at the end of future sessions—and/or in the Extender Session—to see if you've made any progress on answers.)

5. RESPOND 8 minutes

Access the religion section of your local newspaper (or the newspaper from the nearest large city), or bring in a copy. Work with participants to find services of other religions advertised. Also find Web pages of local congregations of Hindu, Buddhist, Islamic, or Jewish faith communities, or use the yellow pages of your local phone book (Look under Religious Organizations and Synagogues, among others.)

Make preliminary plans for one or more field trips related to this study course. Perhaps all you will do is set up a committee to decide who will do what (get information, make contacts, report back to the group). Plan either to visit a service or ask for an on-site presentation.

Who has truth?

- "I don't know what to do with passages like, 'I am the way, the truth, and the life, no one comes to [God] but through me'... but I don't have to be the one to figure it out. That is God's job. I just know that I have to love my sisters and brothers of all beliefs (even if it is atheism). I believe that is Jesus' strongest teaching: 'Love your neighbor as yourself.' Not 'love your *Christian* neighbor as yourself.'"

- "There are elements in other religions that have a basis in truth, just not the whole picture (and I would even say we don't have the whole picture—just the major pieces of it)."

- "Sincerity is important when talking about religious beliefs, but should one try to persuade others? 'What is true and helpful for one person may not be true or helpful for another.'"

Quotes from youth

Note: If distance makes such a field trip impossible, plan instead a time to watch together a DVD or YouTube videos that focus on Hinduism, Buddhism, Islam, or Judaism. (See Introduction.) For example, *Little Buddha* is a film from the early 1990s, starring Keanu Reeves. It chronicles the life of Siddhartha, the young prince who became known as the Buddha.

Now offer a closing statement: *In the sessions ahead, we'll be looking at some of the world's religions. We cannot hope to understand all about these religions, and many of our questions will go unanswered—for now. The key is to be open to learning and to making friends with people of other faiths, which is part of our Christian calling. Contrary to expectation, study of major world religions does not weaken commitment to Jesus. It can instead give us a new appreciation for his uniqueness.*

>>>
LOOK AHEAD

For next session, prepare "Key Hindu Concepts" slips (as described in Explore), and consider the option of doing a video or audio version of the interview with Rakesh.

Also, you'll need a 3-foot (1-meter) length of clothesline rope or heavy string for each person.

INSIGHTS FROM HOLY WRITINGS

>> ### THE "GOD QUESTION" ENCOUNTERS REVELATION...

How shall we view other religions? In Acts 17, Paul encounters a religion in Athens and displays impressive tolerance toward it. On the other hand, he makes it clear that he offers revealed truth that fulfills and supersedes the wisdom these worshipers already have from their speculations and "their own poets." Paul proclaims Christ as a unique incarnation of God—and the resurrection as proof of his claims.

In light of Paul's approach, we must hold two natural tendencies in tension:

- We do wish to accept people who are different, respect other cultures, and give a full hearing to others' sincerely held beliefs. And we welcome the good and the true we find in other religions. We refuse to caricature them when we attempt to explain them (while realizing that we will most surely convey unfortunate distortions).
- But no matter how much we study, who can be thoroughly objective about religion? We approach the question from our own various presuppositions and faith commitments.

Therefore, we *can* learn from others while continuing to affirm, with Paul, the uniqueness of Christ's incarnation and resurrection. Richard Niebuhr proposed the concept of "confessing faith"—we recognize that our theologies *about* God are finite (having historical limitations); only God is absolute. Thus, we can hold firmly to our beliefs while confessing their incompleteness. This opens us to learn from, and dialogue with, other perspectives, where we find space for genuine, sincere witness.

>>>
"The pluralism and the diversity of religions... are willed by God in His wisdom... This divine wisdom is the source from which the right to freedom of belief and the freedom to be different derives."

Pope Francis and Ahmad Al-Tayyeb, *A Document on Human Fraternity for World Peace and Living Together*, 4 February 2019

Contrary to what might be expected, the study of the world religions rarely weakens commitment to Jesus. Rather, it can give us a new appreciation for his uniqueness. The religions come through as philosophies of life, with certain principles being applicable to the *practice* of the Christian faith: such as ego-relinquishment (taught by Jesus), love, or non-violence. However, the historical reality of Jesus and his teachings cuts through to a deeper foundation upon which we build our faith. Christians are not merely ethicists, with effective philosophies of life. They are indwelt, individually and corporately, by the dynamic life of Jesus.

›› HIGHER, DEEPER, FARTHER

Some people studying this topic may well experience...

- **Increased interest in theological inquiry:** By comparing and contrasting one's beliefs with (sometimes radically) different worldviews, they may feel challenged to "bone up" on their own beliefs, and will work at formulating and explaining their own positions.

- **Deeper personal spiritual growth:** Some young people may be inspired by the commitment of religious adherents to such practices as contemplation of God's presence and love, ego-relinquishment, or peace-seeking. They can incorporate such practices as they have been taught in Christian scripture and tradition.

- **Greater effectiveness in reaching out:** Speaking with someone of another religion from a basis of knowledge about the other's beliefs can lay the foundation for a respectful discussion, as well as informed and compassionate service to neighbors.

Exploring tough questions facing youth today

1. Isn't it unfair to judge one religion as right and the others as wrong?
2. Don't all religions teach basically the same thing?
3. If Jesus is the only way, what about those who have never had a chance to hear about him?

Instructions: Choose one or more possibilities under "Possible Insights," and mark its number next to your Big Question if it seems relevant. Be ready to share how the Insights you chose help you answer the question.

Possible Insights:
(Holy Writings, Statements, and Points to Ponder)
Check out these statements and questions. Which ones might help you in a search for answers?

1. What about Abraham? Moses? David? They didn't accept Christ, but did *he* accept *them*? So...must a person necessarily know *about* Christ in order to be part of the Life of God?
2. "Is there injustice on God's part? By no means! For [God] says to Moses, 'I will have mercy on whom I have mercy, and I will have compassion on whom I have compassion.' So it depends not on human will or exertion, but on God, who shows mercy" (Romans 9:14-16).
3. It's true that most religions *share* certain features: (1) belief in the transcendent, (2) a fellowship of believers, (3) a priesthood of some kind, (4) moral principles.
4. "I have other sheep that do not belong to this fold. I must bring them also, and they will listen to my voice. So there will be one flock, one shepherd" (John 10:16).
5. "The heavens are telling the glory of God; and the firmament proclaims his handiwork. Day to day pours forth speech, and night to night declares knowledge.... [Yet] their voice goes out through all the earth, and their words to the end of the world" (Psalm 19:1-4).
6. "When you search for me, you will find me; if you seek me with all your heart" (Jeremiah 29:13).
7. "The true light, which enlightens everyone, was coming into the world" (John 1:9).
8. "For what can be known about God is plain to them, because God has shown it to them. Ever since the creation of the world his eternal power and divine nature, invisible though they are, have been understood and seen through the things he has made. So they are without excuse" (Romans 1:19-20).
9. God is surely more fair than we are! Or else our conception of God is unworthy of God's true nature.
10. Even a Christian cannot *earn* salvation through his or her religion.
11. "For God shows no partiality. All who have sinned apart from the law will also perish apart from the law, and all who have sinned under the law will be judged by the law. For it is not the hearers of the law who are righteous in God's sight, but the doers of the law who will be justified. When Gentiles, who do not possess the law, do instinctively what the law requires, these, though not having the law, are a law to themselves. They show that what the law requires is written on their hearts, to which their own conscience also bears witness; and their conflicting thoughts will accuse or perhaps excuse them on the day when, according to my gospel, God, through Jesus Christ, will judge the secret thoughts of all" (Romans 2:11-16).
12. All human knowledge—about anything—is partial and incomplete.
13. Does sincerely holding to a belief guarantee that it is true?
14. "Long ago God spoke to our ancestors in many and various ways by the prophets, but in these last days he has spoken to us by a Son, whom he appointed heir of all things, through whom he also created the worlds" (Hebrews 1:1-2).

Mantras, Menorahs, and Minarets : Session 1

Permission is granted to photocopy this handout for use with this session.

>>> **SESSION 2**

HINDUSIM—TRY, TRY, TRY, AGAIN? >>>

>>> KEY VERSES

For by grace you have been saved through faith, and this is not your own doing; it is the gift of God—not the result of works, so that no one may boast. (Ephesians 2:8-9)

>>> FAITH STORY

Ephesians 2:1-10

>>> FAITH FOCUS

The apostle Paul wanted the Ephesian faith community to be sure of one thing—they had been blessed by God with great spiritual riches by the divine action of grace, an incomparable gift from God. Now they could live in gratitude and holiness.

In one way of thinking, such an approach to life is "unfair." Our old slate of misdeeds, based on "the passions of our flesh," is wiped clean, and we don't need to keep scrubbing. For Hindus, such unfairness does not exist in reality; justice is always done—through the infallible workings of *karma*.

>>> SESSION GOAL

Introduce participants to Hinduism and the idea of *karma*, and see how it compares and contrasts with Christian grace.

TEACHING PLAN

1. FOCUS 8-10 minutes

Start by introducing a North American teenage Hindu, Rakesh Ramakrishna. Distribute copies of the handout sheet, along with highlighters or pencils. Then say: *Today we're asking, "What is Hinduism?" Perhaps the best way to begin would be to ask Rakesh, who lives in a Hindu family, to explain how he views his religion, and lives it daily.*

Read Rakesh's story aloud (as participants follow along).* Ask them to study Rakesh's baseball story in silence for a moment, then follow the instructions that come after the story, highlighting a phrase or sentence that they might pick up on as a conversation starter if they were actually having a face-to-face conversation with Rakesh.

>>> Materials needed and advance preparation

- Copies of the handout sheet for Session 2 (*optional:* record the story that's on the sheet)

- Highlighter markers or pencils

- Chalkboard/chalk or newsprint/markers

- In advance, photocopy and cut apart the "Key Hindu Concepts" (see Explore and Insights).

- Bibles

- A 3-foot (1-meter) length of clothesline rope or heavy string for each person (Apply, Option A)

- Index cards, optional shoebox (Apply, Option B)

- Choose chant and mantra options (Apply, Option C)

Put these three options on the chalkboard or newsprint, in the typical words your particular group would use. For example:

1. **Wha...Wha...*What???*** (Something you don't understand)
2. **Hey, that's cool.** (something you'd agree with)
3. **No way!** (something you might challenge or dispute)

Test your assumptions about Hinduism by exploring the website:

http://religion.blogs.cnn.com/2014/04/25/9-myths-about-hinduism-debunked/.

2. CONNECT 5-7 minutes

When everyone has highlighted a phrase and chosen one of the three options, ask for volunteers to share why they chose that phrase or sentence. Follow up by asking whether, from the information they can glean in Rakesh's short comment, they can begin to get a picture of what Hinduism is like. Field some comments.

》 ***Option:** Rather than reading Rakesh's statement aloud, contact a group member in advance to record (audio or video) the statement, as if giving a first-person account. Play it twice. Before the second play-back, invite everyone to listen for the phrase or sentence they'd pick up on, as described above. (Of course, if you have a Hindu friend willing to give an interview, go for it!)

Now offer your own "what-I-picked-up-on" choice in Rakesh's story: *Let's focus on Rakesh's interesting statement, "You think it's a coincidence, but it's not." This is a basic description of the concept of* **karma,** *the moral law of cause and effect.*

Discuss:

- *Have you ever wondered whether there is some form of automatic payback system in the universe?*
- *Wouldn't it be fairer if good was always rewarded and bad was always punished?*
- *When did you, personally, wish that this was the case? When did you hope that it wasn't the case?*

3. EXPLORE THE STORIES 15-20 minutes

Shift to this activity by saying: *Hinduism sees that life can only be fair when every good or bad action is balanced by its appropriate reward or punishment. So does that dismiss the need for grace and forgiveness?*

Help your group get a feel for Hinduism, especially the idea of *karma,* and how it compares and contrasts with Christian grace. Deal with the two stories in turn:

The Hindu Story

Depending on the size of your group, pair up or just hand out your "Key Hindu Concepts" slips (from page 16) to individuals. (**Note:** It's okay if some individuals have the same concept. If you have more slips than people, some may volunteer to study more than one key concept.)

Invite people to study the concept for a few minutes and try to get a handle on it so that they will be able to give a brief and clear explanation to the rest of the group, *with a time limit of 35 seconds each!*

》 **Options:** Invite participants to illustrate the picture-concept described on the paper slip, using chalk and a chalkboard and/or markers and newsprint. Alternatively, they could make an animated GIF (a short, looping video) on their phones to illustrate their explanations.

As each individual (or pair) is explaining a key concept to the rest of the group, you, as leader, will supplement with clarifications from the Insights section and your additional study. Sum up each with a few key words or phrases on chalkboard or newsprint. Ask for further questions or comments, putting into a "parking lot" any you can't answer, to let people know you will follow up for next time.

The Christian Story

Now turn to this Bible passage that has bearing on the concept of karma and the Christian message of salvation by grace: Ephesians 2:1-10. Ask someone to read the passage aloud, and then reread verses 8 and 9. Ask: *How would you define "grace"? When did you experience it? How does **grace** compare/contrast with **karma**?*

>> **Option:** Draw this step to a close by suggesting certain ideas in Hinduism that may also be common to Christianity:

- aspirations toward the life of the spirit vs. pursuit of material things—the emphasis on seeing the finiteness of "things" as failing to bring ultimate satisfaction
- the desire for awareness of self (asking: What is its true essence and meaning in the universe?)—seeking quietness, meditation, simplicity of life
- the goal of union with the Absolute (though in Hinduism viewed as an impersonal "absorption," rather than connection with a Creator who loves and cares for each of us)

4. APPLY 10-12 minutes

Choose option A or B to demonstrate and apply the concept of *karma*: the belief that good and bad actions must balance out in order to put an end to *samsara*, every individual's cycle of death and reincarnation. Option C offers practicing a chant or mantra, a key Hindu ritual. If you have time, work with both karma and chant.

>> **Option A:** Hand each person a 1-meter (3-foot) length of clothesline rope or heavy string, and have everyone tie knots in their lengths of rope—one for every sin they've committed. Set a time limit of 4 minutes for them to think and tie.

Then give them a time limit to *untie* the knots, according to how many really good things they've done in their life so far. The time limit is determined like this: Ask up to five people to take a guess as to how many years they think they will live. Add the age guesses together, then divide by five (or however many guesses were made) to arrive at an average age. Then *each year counts as one second of time to untie the knots.*

Begin and let everyone start untying their knots, the **key rule** being: *In order to untie a knot, you must be thinking of a good action you have done* (let them know you'll be asking for examples!).

Call time and find out who still has knots left on their ropes. Ask these people for examples of good actions they have done, which allowed them to untie a sin-knot. Then discuss with the whole group:

- *How would you feel if this really is the way your eventual salvation will be determined?*
- *How many lives do you think you'd have to live in order to wipe out every bad thought or deed produced in this lifetime?*
- *What advantages would there be to this plan of salvation?*
- *What problems might there be—for you?*

>> **Option B:** Divide the group in two, and supply each team with index cards and pencils. Team members sit in a circle, each with several index cards. Each team has about 6 minutes to brainstorm as many challenges as they can and throw into the challenge pile (perhaps a shoebox in the center of the circle).

Instructions:

> *Team #1:* What challenges might a Hindu make to the concept of GRACE (kindness from God we don't deserve)?
>
> *Team #2:* What challenges might a Christian make to the Hindu concept of KARMA (moral balance of cause and effect)?

When time is up, read aloud the entries on the cards and use them as a basis for discussion. Supplement team responses with any or all of these examples of questions/challenges:

Possible challenges to Karma/Hinduism:

1. Isn't it hard to think of living without any forgiveness?
2. Do we really have to do everything on our own? Don't we all need help sometimes to get up when we fall down?
3. Don't you wish for a personal and loving God, since that is what we look for in our human relationships?
4. What reason would you have to try to help someone, since they must be getting what they deserve?

Possible challenges to Grace/Christianity:

1. Isn't grace just another way of saying "unfair"? Why shouldn't a person's every bad deed be punished? Doesn't forgiving someone make God unjust?
2. Isn't your God too small and understandable? (You say: "God thinks this, God does that," etc. Our God is too big to put in a box like that.)
3. Isn't there a loss of mystery in Christianity, since it bases its truth on history and flesh and blood? (That is, Hinduism is transcendent and ultimately unexplainable.)
4. Why do good works, if they don't really earn you a better place in the next life?

>> **Option C: Daily ritual. Recite holy words/Teach a mantra** (a word or sound repeated to aid concentration in meditation). Choose one or more of these audio/written resources to learn or listen to a classic Hindu mantra:

- http://www.freemeditationinfo.com/meditation-instructions/hindu-mantras.html
- http://www.ancientsacredknowledge.com/hindu/om-namah-shivaya/

Additional helps:
- http://www.hinduwebsite.com/rituals.asp
- http://hinduism.about.com/od/basics/u/beliefs_practices.htm (click the link "How To Be an Ideal Hindu")
- http://www.patheos.com/Library/Hinduism/Ritual-Worship-Devotion-Symbolism/Rites-and-Ceremonies.html

LOOK AHEAD

For next session, you'll need pennies, as well as a prize (optional) for the winners of a tug-of-war.

5. RESPOND 3-5 minutes

Say: *Let's get practical. If you were a Hindu, and you saw someone suffering, should you help her? In other words, would you be tampering with the law of **karma** by trying to stop a bad effect of a past cause?* Refer your group members to the story of Rakesh that opened this session, and ask (field some very quick responses): *What would you do and say if your friend landed in the hospital?* If you have time, work in pairs to brainstorm specific responses in terms of words and deeds: (1) what you would *say* as a message of Christian encouragement (refer to Eph. 2:8-9); and (2) what you could *do* as an act of Christian good works (refer to Eph. 2:10).

Close in prayer, asking God to make us one in a spirit of peace.

INSIGHTS FROM HOLY WRITINGS

» KARMA ENCOUNTERS GRACE

David Shenk, a Christian writer, says Hinduism is a "kaleidoscope of beliefs and practices." And indeed, to a Western mind the religion may seem filled with contradictions. On the one hand, viewing the common folk practice of Hinduism we see the worship of over fifty million gods! On the other hand, the philosophy of Vedanta offers the intellectual and mystical-oriented person a voyage into "inner regions," through meditation, towards enlightenment about the oneness of all things. No matter how one practices this faith, there is no doubt that Hinduism is deeply embedded in the history and culture of India.

So the best way to grasp this religion is to lay out the basics of Vedanta, a modern version of the core beliefs made popular in the West at the turn of the twentieth century. The key concept is *karma*.

Karma, as a law of nature, makes everything balance out in the moral realm. Thus Hindus would look at the Christian concept of forgiveness of sin as an ill-considered attempt to sidestep the rules of the moral universe. Why would we want to do that—to break the immediate relationship between action and consequence, a relationship which must surely exist for the universe to be just? As Shenk says: "Forgiveness or merit acquired from another source is a dangerous idea. [It] does not fit the Hindu worldview, which believes that nothing can bend or detract from the inevitability of destiny determined by one's actions."

Karma:

Basically, it's the law of cause and effect, played out in a life through a person's many births and rebirths. Every action (cause) produces an effect, which remains after the action. Each time we die, we take with us the leftover effect of each finished or unfinished action. When we are reborn, all the energy of our good and bad actions follows us into the new lifetime. Everything that is happening now is the result of our previous actions (causes). And, the actions (causes) we take now shape our future lives.

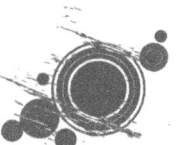

» TOUGH QUESTIONS

One of the social effects of this philosophy is a kind of fatalism. If one's place in life is predetermined by a long series of deaths and rebirths, why strive for improvement? One's caste-duties must be performed as best as possible until the next birth takes place. If another person is suffering, would it really be proper to stop the "payment" of *karma* by trying to stop the suffering?

Just as Christian theology has wrestled with its tough questions over the centuries, including its own version of Lutheran and Calvinist predestination, so is Hindu thought also evolving. Religious philosopher Sarvepalli Radhadrishnan (1888-1975) wrote, "Hinduism has through the centuries been a religion of destiny and submission. A man's [sic] future was written on his forehead at his birth, and this is something that cannot be changed either by God or man.... This will not do for young Indians today. The modern Hindu believes that, within limits at least, man's destiny is in his own hands, and that he is called to strive and to achieve." (Quoted in Stephen Neill's *Christian Faith and Other Faiths*)

Neill himself muses, "The tragic death of Mahatma Gandhi at the hands of an assassin might be fitted into the traditional framework of suffering in this life as retribution for sins committed in a previous existence. But the veneration for the Mahatma felt by millions of his fellow countrymen makes it seem to me unlikely that they would see in his death anything other than suffering endured as the consequence of, or as expiation for, the sins of others."

» WISDOM FOR TODAY...

In Hinduism, individuality is an illusion to overcome. But personality is important to youth! They are often trying to improve it, change it, or cope with it.

Point out that the goal of both Hinduism and Christianity is unity with the Eternal. However, note the difference. According to Ephesians 2, we are called into relationship with a personal God in order to experience God's kindness forever (v. 7). If unity is sought, it is not so much a unity of *being* as of *relationship*. Christians know that who they are is valued by God and that their being is fulfilled as it becomes more Christlike, in each individual's particular tones.

Key Hindu Concepts

Photocopy and cut out enough of these slips for your group members to use in Explore.

Cut apart on this line ✂ --

Brahman: The absolute, undivided essence of being/reality; essence of all living things. Pure existence. All is God! (But humans often don't recognize this oneness of all things.)
Key Picture: Imagine different objects made out of clay: tree, person, rock, dog, car, etc. They appear to be different things, but they are really all the same *substance*. You could lump them together and the differences would disappear. All is clay.

Cut apart on this line ✂ --

Maya: The obscuring quality in the universe that makes us think there are individual beings, including ourselves. It's the illusion of individuality. It's our ignorance, the reason we have trouble recognizing the oneness of all things. Therefore, we compete with one another; we have our egos, our desires, and our dissatisfaction.
Key Picture: Dirt on a window pane. We can't see the sun clearly because our vision of the real scene is clouded.

Cut apart on this line ✂ --

Samsara: The round-and-round cycle of death and rebirth over countless ages of time. This is the penalty for our ignorance. We are tied down to a round of births, deaths, and rebirths into a higher or lower class of being.
Key Picture: Two vertical funnel clouds, connected at their narrowest ends: one swirls upward, the other spirals downward. As we are reborn, our *karma* (the effects of our good or bad actions) follows us and we go higher or lower in the scale of creatures seeking release from the cycle.

Cut apart on this line ✂ --

Karma: Basically, it's the law of cause and effect, played out in a life through a person's many births and rebirths. Every action (cause) produces an effect, which remains after the action. Each time we die we take with us the leftover effect of each finished or unfinished action. When we are reborn, all the energy of our good and bad actions follows us into the new lifetime. Everything that is happening now is the result of our previous actions (causes). And, the actions (causes) we take now shape our future lives.
Key Picture: Tying and untying knots in a rope over the millennia of rebirths.

Cut apart on this line ✂ --

Caste: Four large divisions of people, originally based on skin color. Nowadays there are hundreds of castes, based on family background, employment, community, etc. Each caste has its particular duties to perform in order to create good karma. One must advance from lower to higher, more spiritually privileged, castes through reincarnation.
Key Picture: Grades in a school, with hundreds of grades between best and worst.

Cut apart on this line ✂ --

Rebirth: The other side of the coin of *karma*. The soul migrates from one existence to the other after the physical death of the body, in order to keep working off the effects of bad *karma* by balancing it with good *karma* (law of cause and effect). A person who is mostly bad will be reborn into a lower caste or state, perhaps as an animal, or even a blade of grass. The process takes eons of time. The highest caste is the *Brahmin*, or the priestly caste. This caste is the closest to reaching *Moksha*—the end of rebirths.
Key Picture: Look at a photo of yourself as a child. Is that YOU? But it is a different body! You have to ask: What part is ME? What part is present now? In some way the real you has moved into a new form of existence (taken up residence in a new body).

Cut apart on this line ✂ --

Atman: The essence of each person, which, because of *maya* (illusion), is thought of as separate and individual. However, the great truth of Hinduism, for those who are enlightened, is that there is no separation between the person and all other things; *Brahman* (the Absolute) and *Atman* are the same. Each individual *Atman*, while existing in *maya* (illusion), is trying to return to its true identity as *Brahman*.
Key Picture: Sparks from a fire. They appear as separate entities, but they are actually one thing: fire.

Cut apart on this line ✂ --

Yoga: Physical and mental practices aimed at uniting body, mind, and spirit. Intended to calm and discipline the constant activity of thought in order to sense the true reality of *Brahman-Atman* oneness; that is, I and the Absolute are one. This recognition is the moment of enlightenment.
Key Picture: Stilling of the waves on a crystal-clear lake. In rough waters we see only fragments of images. But when the surface is calm, we can look down to the wholeness of the sandy bottom. The effects of *maya* (illusion) are reduced as one gains skill in experiencing oneness.

Cut apart on this line ✂ --

Moksha: Final salvation! The bliss of the final reabsorption of one's being into Being Itself (the Absolute, World Soul, or *Brahman*). This occurs upon being enlightened to your true identity and exhausting the effects of *karma* through the ages of rebirths. Now there is no more individual consciousness to suffer and compete.
Key Picture: A drop of water is released into a glass of water.

Baseball, Hot Dogs, and... KARMA!

Rakesh Ramakrishna, a 15-year-old baseball fan, is a high school sophomore in Baltimore. Here's what he says about his religion:

There are lots of things to know about being Hindu, you know? Lots of gods and stuff, and prayers to say. But I think there's a real practical side, too. Because you can understand why things happen and not get so upset about them.

You know, like my friend who plays on my team at school—he's Catholic. Anyway, he slides into second base the first game of the season and really rips his knee up. He had to have surgery on it and now his season is over. I went to visit him, and he said he couldn't figure out why this freak accident had to happen to him. He's all upset and worried. I just told him: "Hey, you gotta start trying to make more good energy in your life, so maybe these bad things won't happen so much."

He looked at me kinda funny, but the thing is, when something bad happens to you, you think it's a coincidence, but it's not. It's bad energy from your past lives just balancing out in your life right now. You can't change that, so you might as well accept it.

Instructions: Highlight one phrase or sentence that you'd pick up on as a conversation starter if you were having a face-to-face conversation with Rakesh. The phrase or sentence might (1) raise a question you'd ask; or (2) cause a comment of agreement; or (3) cause a comment of disagreement.

Permission is granted to photocopy this handout for use with this session.

››› SESSION 3

BUDDHISM—HOW DO WE HANDLE SUFFERING? ›››

›› KEY VERSES

Beloved, do not be surprised at the fiery ordeal that is taking place among you to test you, as though something strange were happening to you. But rejoice insofar as you are sharing Christ's sufferings, so that you may also be glad and shout for joy when his glory is revealed. (1 Peter 4:12-13)

›› FAITH STORY

1 Peter 4:12-19

›› FAITH FOCUS

The apostle Peter addresses a church filled with non-Jews who may well be shocked at the prospect of suffering persecution. (This would not have been surprising to the Jews!)

Peter tries to assure them that, for a Christian, life involves pain and they will inevitably share in the suffering Jesus endured as a result of his teachings and manner of living. Yet suffering is redeemed—fiery ordeals can test faith and make it stronger.

›› SESSION GOAL

Explore with participants the contrast between finding an escape from suffering (Buddhism) and Christianity—which points to suffering (particularly on the cross) as the means of redemption and strengthened faith.

›› Materials needed and advance preparation

- Pennies (one for every two people)
- Writing paper and pencils
- Chalkboard/chalk or newsprint/markers
- Bibles (various translations)
- Copies of the handout sheet for Session 3, highlighters
- Yarn, optional prize for tug-of-war winners (Apply, Option A)
- Index cards, small box or container (Apply, Option A)
- Download and print (if necessary) a meditation to use (Apply, Option B)

TEACHING PLAN

1. FOCUS 8-12 minutes

Pair up. Hand each pair a penny, along with paper and pencil, so they can jot the results of ten coin-tosses each. Say: *Suppose you could predict your future with coin-tosses! Heads is the total amount of pleasure you are going to have in your life. Tails is the amount of pain and suffering you're going to experience. How will life be for you?*

One partner keeps score while the other tosses. Then switch roles. After the tosses, tally the results for each partner. Follow up by asking:

- *Is anyone here going to live a life that is totally pain-free?*
- *Who's going to have the most pleasure? Most pain?*
- *In your opinion, what are the odds of getting through a whole life with no suffering?*
- *How true-to-life would you say this coin-toss was for you, personally, in terms of the amount of suffering—including emotional suffering—you actually experience in your life? (Ask for percentages.)*
- *Have you ever attempted to stack the odds so you could **avoid** emotional pain? How?*
- *If humans were offered a way to be pain-free in this life, do you think that would be attractive to teens? WHY?*

What about SUFFERING??

- It is not fair; it should be stopped.
- It happens for a reason. If someone is hurting, then someone else must be to blame for it. One option: Take any potentially guilty party to court!
- It is something that can happen to people when they are not shrewd enough to avoid it.

2. CONNECT 5 minutes

Now invite people to list (and jot on the chalkboard or newsprint) every product they can think of that would help a person avoid pain, or numb it. Examples: Tylenol, alcohol, Mineral Ice, cortisone, marijuana, pain-numbing creams, lidocaine, etc.

Very briefly field some responses to:

- *What kinds of pain-numbing products—or techniques—have you used? WHY?*
- *What would be the advantages and benefits of not having these products?*

3. EXPLORE THE STORIES 15-20 minutes

Shift to this activity by saying: *Our human freedom creates the possibility for suffering—a big problem for human beings, right? Let's take a look at Buddhism, which offers an alternative to suffering. But first, what does the Bible say?*

The Bible's Story

Read 1 Peter 4:12-19 aloud, in various versions, as participants follow along. Then ask: *How would you summarize, in one sentence **that a third-grader could understand**, the apostle Peter's view of suffering?*

If these points did not emerge, wrap up the discussion by summarizing: *Can good come from suffering? Peter paints a picture of refining metal to make it pure. Faith can be purified and clarified by suffering, and we understand better what it is to follow a Master who gave his life to open life for us.*

Then choose one of the following options for encountering Buddhism:

Buddhism's Story

Option A: Have participants skim "The Story of Buddhism" on the handout sheet, "Siddhartha: From Prince to Preacher," for 3 minutes, highlighting one statement or phrase that raises questions for them.

Then decide whether to tell the story or use the handout as a read-along. Let participants know that you are not an expert on Buddhism (unless you are!), and that much about this religion will have to be left for further study.

Clarify as best you can any points given on the sheet. Then discuss:

- *In your opinion, what things do Buddhism and Christianity have in common when they talk about human suffering?*
- *What is the sharpest contrast that stands out to you?*

Explore more about Buddhism with Marcus Borg's book **Jesus and Buddha,** or at http://buddhanet.net/e-learning/5minbud.htm.

- *If Jesus and Siddhartha were to have a conversation about the nature and purpose of suffering, what do you think Siddhartha would say? How might Jesus respond?*

Invite sharing of any of their highlighted phrases that still raise questions. When everyone has had a chance to respond, summarize: *The point is, everybody hurts, and suffering is unavoidable in life—both Buddhism and Christianity agree there! But according to Christianity, it's NOT based on how good we are, or aren't, or on how well we get rid of our desires by learning to ignore them. In other words, if you are suffering, it doesn't mean that you are necessarily at fault. You can do everything right, and still hurt.*

》》 **Option B:** View a 15-minute YouTube introduction to Buddhism's view of suffering by Thich Nhat Hanh, https://youtu.be/OtZtR9BKDYk, or preview and choose a similar portion of an introduction by the Dalai Lama, https://www.youtube.com/watch?v=rWDiyGAOKk4.

4. APPLY 8-10 minutes

》》 **Option A: Tug-of-War.** Divide into two teams, and set up as if you were going to have a traditional tug-of-war, *except* for this catch—use a long piece of yarn for your rope. Explain that each side will try to win by pulling the others across the line, as usual (make a good prize available). However, if the yarn breaks, *both sides lose*.

LOOK AHEAD

Prepare a posterboard or newsprint for "promise graffiti" for next session (see Focus).

Gather supplies for a **Shabbat service** (described in Apply, *Option B*).

Also, if you think your group will need extra help with the timeline activity in Explore, gather or access a few sample Bible timelines.

The contest will probably be a short one! Use it to highlight the potential value of loosening our grip on what we intensely desire. Say: *We've seen that Buddhism prescribes "detachment" as a response to suffering in life. Let's see how we might detach from, or let go of, things that cause us suffering.*

Have everyone sit in a circle, distribute several index cards to each person, and ask them to jot on each card **one thing** teens can get overly attached to. After a few minutes of writing, place all the cards in a small container, shuffle, and pass the container around, with each participant taking one card. Now go around the circle and ask each person to tell:

A. *How attached are you, personally, to this thing—to either avoid pain or increase pleasure?*

B. *If not THIS thing, what is it that you could stand to loosen your grip on a bit?*

》》 **Option B: Ritual practice: Meditation.** Lead the group in a meditation based on a YouTube meditation such as https://www.youtube.com/watch?v=kZA_R3sQFzY (as leader, you read the words while participants close eyes), or choose a guided meditation, such as https://www.youtube.com/watch?v=1-OdUkAFWtk.

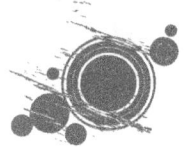

5. RESPOND 5 minutes

Now ask everyone to sit back to back with their original coin-toss partner. Say: *We are not alone in our suffering; we can lean on God and one another for help. Offer a silent prayer for the person whose back is leaning against yours. You may not know this person's deepest pain. But God does. Ask the Life-Giver for encouragement and peace in this brother or sister's week ahead.*

As the teens continue to sit back to back, offer this wrap-up: *Suffering is usually a sign that something is wrong, and turning your back on the suffering won't help right the wrong. Facing the suffering will. In order to know peace in our lives, we must learn how to breathe through our pain, with God's help.*

"Although the world is full of suffering, it is full also of the overcoming of it."

Helen Keller

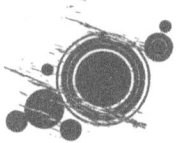

For a much fuller set of parallel sayings of Jesus and Buddha, see Marcus Borg's book of the same title. The book also addresses the mystery of how these two, living centuries as well as continents apart, could teach such similar truths.

INSIGHTS FROM HOLY WRITINGS

DO WE HAVE TO HURT?

Can good flow from suffering? Peter's use of the word "fiery" in verse 12 conveys the picture of refining metal to make it pure. Like refining metal, faith can be purified and clarified by suffering, and we understand better what it is to follow a Master who gave his life to open life for us.

Traditional theology says that evil and pain came into the world through human choice, but that God came to share in the suffering with us, and to redeem it. The cross is the Christian's ultimate answer to the problem of pain. An eternal person taking upon himself the pain and alienation of the world and coming through it into resurrection renders suffering powerless to defeat the human being.

How does Buddhism view the problem? For the Buddhist, pain and suffering, though to be expected, are a result of wrong perceptions, which must be changed. Getting caught up in pain is an indication of the worst human condition: remaining attached to the world of illusion, as though things and people had any substance at all. Consider this set of contrasts:

Buddhism	Christianity
1. Detachment from thought (a veil) is the way to immediacy of experience. (Through meditation we can correct wrong perceptions of the mind that seek to interpret everything as good or bad. There just *is*.)	1. Rational thought (a tool) is the way to greater understanding of experience.
2. Suffering as wholly evil (to be escaped). (See the story of the Buddha.)	2. Suffering as potentially significant and/or atoning (to be transformed).
3. Love as contemplation of goodwill toward all beings (passionless benevolence).	3. *Agape* as passionate action and engagement on behalf of others (sympathetic compassion).
4. Look to self alone for attaining nirvana (emptiness/extinction of self).	4. Look to God alone for receiving salvation (wholeness/fulfillment of self).

Here is how the Dalai Lama has compared the Buddha and Christ:

> "Love and compassion are common to all faith traditions. Compassion for all sentient beings made by your Creator, this is integral to Christianity. Christians strive to fulfill the wishes of your Creator, and the primary wish of your Creator is love, is that not so? The Buddha and the Christ were similar men: ascetics, men used to hardship and not to luxury, men of perseverance and effort, extraordinary teachers. And indeed such hardship and ascetic practice are common to all the great spiritual teachers of the world. Yet now we seem to believe that our intellectual progress has advanced us past the great teachers of the past; we seem to believe we are superior to the simple teachers of long ago. But this is a mistake on our part."

And here is a summary of the place of suffering in the Christian life, from C. S. Lewis' *The Problem of Pain*:

> "The Christian doctrine of suffering explains, I believe, a very curious fact about the world we live in. The settled happiness and security which we all desire, God withholds from us by the very nature of the world: but joy, pleasure, and merriment He has scattered broadcast. We are never safe, but we have plenty of fun, and some ecstasy. It is not hard to see why. The security we crave would teach us to rest our hearts in this world and pose an obstacle to our return to God: a few moments of happy love, a landscape, a symphony, a merry meeting with our friends, a bath or a football match, have no such tendency. Our Father refreshes us on the journey with some pleasant inns, but will not encourage us to mistake them for home."

>> WISDOM FOR TODAY...

The topic of suffering is not an easy one for any of us. Obviously, Siddhartha (the Buddha) suffered greatly in his life, just seeking out the meaning of suffering. Youth may look at this topic in very practical ways, asking: *Why is life so unfair?* Perhaps all you can do is affirm that the question about suffering is one of the greatest questions anyone can ask. Point out that many people have given their lives in extending compassion to those whose suffering is greater than their own. This is a worthy calling for a Christian, the essence of the kind of *agape* love that has been shown to us. Some people, who have plumbed the depths of pain in their personal experience, have even concluded that a deeper question eventually emerges: *Why is there any **good** in the world at all? And why so much grace?*

Someone once asked the Buddha, "Are you God?" Buddha answered, "No." Then they asked, "An angel?" Again Buddha said, "No." "A saint?" "No." "Then what?"

Buddha smiled and answered, "I am awake!"

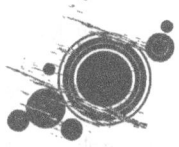

Siddhartha: From Prince to Preacher

Exploring tough questions facing youth today

Unlike Hindus, Buddhists can look back to history for specifics about how their religion began. Around 560 B.C.E., a man named Siddhartha (who eventually became known by the title "the Buddha," meaning "enlightened one") was born into royal wealth and privilege as a Hindu prince. Legend says that before his birth a seer predicted that he would either become a great political leader or—if he ever came to see the suffering in life—a religious leader, one who would bring salvation to all humankind.

Siddhartha's father did not want his son to become a religious leader, so he tried to shield the young prince from ever encountering life's suffering. He was sheltered in the lap of luxury, living in a beautiful palace, surrounded by lovely women, fed the best of food, clothed in fine linens. He spent his days walking and riding his horse through lush, green parks.

But one day, nearing his thirtieth birthday, as he was riding in a park outside the palace gates, Siddhartha encountered four men, one after the other: One was horribly sick, covered with sores; the next was an old man, tottering on his cane; the next was a dead man—a rotting corpse—being carried to his grave. Finally, Siddhartha came across a monk who had renounced the world and simply begged for his food, day by day. This man seemed happy and at peace.

The sudden revelation of life's suffering made Siddhartha realize that he could no longer live his luxurious, sheltered existence. So late one night he kissed his wife and child good-bye and rode off into the wilderness. He removed his fine clothes, cut off his long hair, and wandered for five years seeking the answer to life's pain. He went to great lengths of self-denial, starving himself, allowing the filth and vermin to accumulate on his body, his clothes rotting away. It is said that he became so thin that when he touched his stomach, he was feeling his backbone!

Then one day, overcome by exhaustion and weakness, he fell into a stream of cold water. The shock of the water revived him and he saw that his self-torture was not the answer. He got up, washed himself, put on clothes, and went to a nearby tavern to have a meal.
Then he went to sit under a fig tree to meditate.

For forty days and nights he sat, until the answer came, and, in a flash of insight, he became "the enlightened one." He saw a vision of the endless cycle of birth and death and rebirth. He realized that all people were bound to that endless cycle by one thing: *tanha*, desire. Furthermore, he saw that when he ceased to desire, he was free of all things. Thus he was enlightened, and this was the profound insight Siddhartha would preach to his *sangha* (the community of his faithful followers, composed of monks and lay people). His message came to be known as the **Four Noble Truths**:

1. **All of life is suffering.** To exist is to be unhappy, for we see all around us that everything is constantly in a state of decay. If we wait long enough, even the most durable of physical materials will all return to dust—including, of course, every human body.

2. **The cause of suffering is *tanha*, selfish desire and craving.** Everyone is always looking for something more. No one is content with the here and now. This tendency of humans always to search out the greener pasture is the source of all pain.

3. **The cure for suffering is to eliminate desire.** It can be done! And only in this way can a person be released from the endless round of reincarnation. Only in this way will he or she experience *nirvana*, the extinguishing of personality. Just as the flame of a candle can be blown out, so one enters the Great Void, or Empty Circle.

4. **The way to eliminate desire is to follow the Noble Eightfold Path.** Controlling our behavior shows our determination to reach our goal. Therefore Buddhist missionary preachers spread the word about a system of ridding oneself of *tanha* through correct living:

- **Right viewpoint** (example: understanding illness, how it happens, how to be released from it)
- **Right aspiration** (example: renouncing attachment to the world)
- **Right speech** (example: no lying or abusive talk)
- **Right action** (example: no taking of life, living a simple lifestyle)
- **Right livelihood** (example: having a job that does not support war)
- **Right effort** (example: using one's mind to produce "good *karma*," which will lead to a shorter cycle of rebirths)
- **Right mindfulness** (example: retaining awareness and acceptance of the here and now rather than craving something better in the future)
- **Right concentration** (example: seeking solitude, meditating, enjoying peace of mind)

The Buddha is said to have died many years after his enlightenment, due to eating some poisoned mushrooms. He had begun life as a Hindu prince; he ended it as a preacher of a new way of being: Buddhism, the way of the enlightened ones. His final words to his followers were, "Subject to decay are all component things. Strive earnestly to work out your own salvation."

Mantras, Menorahs, and Minarets : Session 3

Permission is granted to photocopy this handout for use with this session.

>>> **SESSION 4**

JUDAISM—IS THE PROMISE ALIVE? >>>

>> KEY VERSES

"I will make of you a great nation, and I will bless you, and make your name great, so that you will be a blessing." (Genesis 12:2)

Just as Abraham "believed God, and it was reckoned to him as righteousness," so, you see, those who believe are the descendants of Abraham. (Galatians 3:6-7)

"I ask, then, has God rejected his people? By no means! I myself am an Israelite, a descendant of Abraham, a member of the tribe of Benjamin. "(Romans 11:1)

>> FAITH STORY

Genesis 12:1-4; 13:14-18 and Galatians 3:6-9/Romans 4 and 11

>> FAITH FOCUS

Abraham, a Gentile living in the desert, heard the call of God: "Move your family to another place to live!" Along with that challenge came some marvelous promises: Abraham would be given a land for his own, his family would eventually grow into a countless multitude, and his people would be blessed by God and become a source of blessing to others through the ages. So Abraham headed off for this promised land and its blessing.

The Christian story connects followers of Jesus with Abraham and Sarah as their spiritual ancestors. But does that mean that we take over where the Hebrews left off, as though the Jews now have no place in God's plans? "By no means!" states the apostle Paul. "God has not rejected his people whom he foreknew." (Romans 11:1-2)

>> SESSION GOAL

Help participants appreciate the Jewish roots of Christianity, and understand where the two diverge.

>> Materials needed and advance preparation

- In advance, write the words "A PROMISE IS..." in the center of a large piece of posterboard (or newsprint), and hang it on a wall.

- Colored markers or crayons

- Prepare index cards, as described in Explore, *Option A*

- Newsprint/markers or chalkboard/chalk

- Bibles and sample Bible event timelines

- Gather supplies for a Shabbat service (Apply, *Option B*)

- Copies of the handout sheet for Session 4 (Apply, *Option B*)

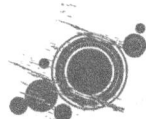

TEACHING PLAN

1. FOCUS 8-10 minutes

Promise Graffiti. Before the session, write the words "A PROMISE IS..." in the center of a large piece of posterboard (or newsprint), and hang it on a wall; then hand out colored

> "On this account the Church cannot forget that she received the revelation of the Old Testament by way of that people whom God in his inexpressible mercy established the ancient covenant... Since Christians and Jews have such a common spiritual heritage, this sacred Council wishes to encourage and further mutual understanding and appreciation."
>
> *Declaration on the Relation of the Church to Non-Christian Religions*, 4.

markers or crayons as participants enter the meeting room. (Or simply use the chalkboard and pieces of colored chalk.)

When everyone has gathered, ask them to let their minds and feelings "wrap around" the idea of PROMISE. "Tag" the poster with creative words, phrases, doodles, or symbols—all are fair game, as well as humor, if respectful, to represent "promise." Let participants know there will be opportunity to tell about their graffiti later. (**Suggestion:** If your group is large, hang several graffiti posters on different walls. If possible, let the posters hang on the wall until the group meets again.)

2. CONNECT 5-8 minutes

As the group finishes up the graffiti, follow up by discussing:

- *Recall a time when you were promised something and you got exactly what you were hoping for. Share that story.*
- *What about a time when you **didn't** get what was promised? What happened?*
- *What part did **waiting** play in these stories?*
- *What do promises, hope, and waiting have to do with your faith?*
- *How are you a blessing to others?*

3. EXPLORE THE STORIES 20 minutes

Shift to this activity by saying: *Judaism is based on promises related to historical events. Let's find out about that history...*

Judaism is very different from the Eastern religions of Hinduism and Buddhism. It is broader than a philosophy. It is a culture, a people, a story of salvation history, as well as a religion. For Jews, God is revealed through the events that take place in history rather than only through "inner enlightenment." This is truly a radical idea!

Understanding Judaism means understanding the history of the Hebrew people—and their waiting for the fulfillment of God's promises to them. How much do you know about this history? We find it in our Old Testament, which Jews call *Tanach* (Law, Prophets, Writings) or simply the Bible.

Choose one of the options below to further introduce the group to Judaism:

>> **Option A:** Hand out the "Periods of History" cards (see page 28) so that everyone in the group has one or more. Then spread out the "Bible, Book, and People" cards at random on a table or on the floor. Tell the group they will have 5 minutes to mingle, to find out what is on everyone's card, and then to use their current knowledge of Hebrew history to assemble themselves in a "timeline" of correct chronological order. (If you think your group might not have enough background, suggest they use the table of contents and timelines in a Bible, or find information online. Together, the group will: (1) link the "Periods of History" cards with the "Bible, Book, and People" cards, and (2) arrange themselves in chronological order. When they are lined up, check how closely they came to the right chronology. If needed, rearrange people, then have everyone sit down in this order.

Note: If you have fewer than 14 people in your group, just have the group work at pairing up the two sets of cards and arranging the cards—instead of themselves—in the correct chronological order. If you have more than 14, also hand out as many "Bible, Book, and People" cards as you need, until everyone has a card. (Scatter the rest on table or floor.) People with "Bible, Book, and People" cards will link arms with the appropriate "Period of History" people as they get into chronological order.

Now, beginning with the first period of Jewish history, invite participants to name anything they know about this particular period. Supplement with your own information, and read a scripture passage or pertinent points from the Insights section, jotting the history-headings on the chalkboard as you go.

Conclude this step by having everyone turn in their Bibles to Genesis 12:1-4 and 17:6 to review the three parts of the promise to Abraham and Sarah. Say: *This is the hope of Judaism—the promise of three things to occur in history: land, seed, and blessing. In this history are the roots of Christianity!* Now read Galatians 3:6-9 and discuss:

- *What evidence of Jewish "roots" do you see in the Christian church today and in yourself, as a spiritual descendant of Abraham and Sarah?*

>> **Option B:** Use one or both of these YouTube videos for the introduction to Judaism:

- https://youtu.be/HyEaAcPGAhA (5 min.) Overview of main historical events.
- https://youtu.be/buhBtLWzSUU (6 min.) Rabbi Berel Wein teaches about core beliefs and frameworks of Judaism, and what makes it different from other religions. Compares Judaism, Islam, and Christianity.

4. APPLY 5-7 minutes

>> **Option A:** Direct everyone's attention back to the graffiti poster (from Focus). Ask:

- *In your opinion, how important would "promise" be in the faith of a Jew?*
- *Should promise and hope be more or less important to Christians today? In what ways?*
- *When you think of your own life with God, what do you **need**? What are you **waiting** for? What is **hopeful**? What is **discouraging**?*

Ask everyone to turn to Romans 4 in their Bibles and to listen as you read verses 1-16. Repeat verse 16, and wrap up this step by pointing out that, according to the apostle Paul, we share the faith of Abraham and Sarah! We, too, are waiting for the blessing, the Messiah to come, but for us it is the second time. With our Jewish neighbors, we wait and hope.

>> **Option B: Ritual experience: Shabbat service.** Invite a Jewish person to lead a Sabbath, or Shabbat, service for the group. Coordinate with this person in advance about what materials you will need to provide. You may need to supply candles, cups, wine or grape juice, and challah (a special egg bread). Use the handout sheet provided at the end of this lesson, or create a different worship aid in coordination with the person who will be leading the service.

Observant Jews keep the Sabbath from sundown on Friday to sundown on Saturday every week, beginning and ending with Sabbath prayers. The handout outlines prayers and actions that take place just before the Friday evening meal is served.

Remember, this is a *Jewish* prayer, and part of their sacred tradition. It is important to take your lead from your Jewish guest as to how to go about this in a way that is respectful of their tradition.

5. RESPOND 8-10 minutes

Begin drawing your session to a close by saying something like: *One important response to any study of Judaism is to focus on the problem of anti-Semitism that has plagued the Jews down through history, including the Nazi Holocaust.* Point out that anti-Semitism is always a danger, even today. We ourselves must be sure to respond with openness, tolerance, and compassion.

Hate crimes against Jews and courageous tolerance coexist:

The news recently carried the story of a Jewish and Christian neighborhood as the season of Hanukkah and Christmas approached:

While the Christians decorated with trees and colored lights, the Jews lit a menorah (candelabra) and set it in the window. One night, the windows in the Jewish home were broken out, and anti-Semitic graffiti was sprayed on the walls. Shocked that such a crime could happen in their neighborhood, one of the Christians responded the next night by placing a menorah in her own window, and many others soon followed the lead. Christmas trees and menorahs stood side by side for the whole season.

LOOK AHEAD

For next session, prepare five rolled-up pieces of newsprint with scrambled Islamic Pillar-statements, as described in Explore, *Option A*.

Also look at Apply, *Option A*, and decide how you want to prepare a bottle of drinking water; whether it is pure water or mixed with salt.

If you are using the Extender Session after the next session, make any necessary plans now.

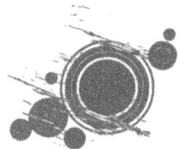

"[The Church] deplores all hatreds, persecutions, displays of anti-semitism leveled at any time or from any source against the Jews."

Declaration on the Relation of the Church to Non-Christian Religions, 4.

Search (or have participants search) online for current incidences of anti-Semitism. Share the stories, and discuss:

- Why do you think such incidences still occur? Why such hatred?
- What evidence of anti-Semitism do you see in your community or school?

Close by asking for a commitment: to fight anti-Semitism, seeing that Judaism is the foundation of Christian faith, and that Jewish people are still messengers in our world of God's holiness and hope.

INSIGHTS FROM HOLY WRITINGS

CHRISTIANITY ENCOUNTERS ITS ROOTS

Judaism is one of the three theocentric (God-at-the-center) religions, along with Christianity and Islam. Both of the other two religions have roots in Judaism. When people use the word Judaism, they may be referring to a history, a culture, a religion, or a people. As a religion, Judaism is remarkable in at least four ways when compared with other religions:

1. *It is not in the least speculative.* Contrasted with Hinduism, for instance, which even though it has its "characters"—such as Krishna and Arjuna in the *Bhagavad Gita*—these avatars (incarnations of Hindu deities) are never assumed to have had real historical existences. But Judaism finds its roots in the humans Abraham and Sarah, Jacob and Rachel. They are real people, who walked the desert sands and felt the sun on their faces.

2. *Judaism's God, Yahweh, is an active Providence, watching over one small nation.* Only gradually did the understanding develop that Yahweh is God of all the earth. Thus, for Judaism, the history of the Hebrews is of supreme importance. God-as-revealed-in-events is more emphasized than God revealed in inner experience.

3. *Yahweh is a moral personality.* Warren Matthews writes in *World Religions*: "The summit of experience for the Hebrews under Moses was the receiving of the commandments of God, given by God to Moses on the top of Mount Sinai, where the covenant between God and his people was renewed. If the Hebrews would serve God exclusively, they would receive a promised land and become a great nation. If they accepted the promise, they had obligations to fulfill that were moral, ceremonial, and cultural. All life was to be lived under the command of God, a theocracy."

4. *Judaism proclaims a personal relationship with God based on covenant and promise.* Hebrew scripture strives to answer this question: Why do the wicked prosper? Hinduism and Buddhism address this question, too, mainly through helping their adherents change their view of reality (to see that things really *aren't* unjust after all; we simply need a truer perspective). But Judaism's "answer" is radically different: Human sin has broken connection with God, and it is a genuine rift, with painful consequences. The alienation can only be overcome through repentance and renewed obedience. God is served in righteousness. The promise of the future realm of peace then becomes real and vibrant once again.

CHRISTIANITY IS ROOTED IN JUDAISM

The apostle Paul declares an unbreakable continuity: We are all blessed by Abraham's and Sarah's stories because we are their spiritual descendants. In fact, Christianity began as a sect of Judaism, and the earliest disciples were mostly practicing Jews (as was Jesus himself) meeting in synagogues. Scripture records the first splits between Judaism and Christianity in the middle of the first century, when first Peter and then Paul invited non-Jews into the church. Even today there are small groups of "Messianic Jews" around the world—Jews who converted to Christianity. This makes the connection Paul spoke of even more vivid.

Yet the other connection is perhaps the most obvious, and the least attractive. The concentration camps of the Nazi Holocaust attest that at least one part of the Gentile world in the middle of the twentieth century attempted not only to divorce itself from Abraham and Sarah's people, but tried to annihilate them. No Jew will forget this, nor must any of us forget.

Viktor Frankl was an Austrian psychologist who suffered and endured the Nazi camps. He epitomized human resilience in his famous book, *Man's Search for Meaning*. He wrote, "What is to give light must endure burning."

WISDOM FOR TODAY...

Today's young people normally seek to get along. But hate crimes are still all too prevalent, and if youth do not have much opportunity to interact with Jews as neighbors, they may unwittingly perpetuate and participate in stereotyping.

The great Jewish theologian Martin Buber sums up the divergence and connection of Christianity and Judaism (in *Israel and the World*): "To you the book is a forecourt; to us it is the sanctuary. But in this place we can dwell together, and together listen to the voice that speaks here.... Your expectation is directed toward a second coming, ours to a coming which has not been anticipated by a first. To you the phrasing of world history is determined by one absolute midpoint, the year nought; to us it is an unbroken flow of tones following each other without a pause from their origin to their consummation. But we can wait for the advent of the One together, and there are moments when we may prepare the way before him together."

"Periods of History" cards	"Bible, Book, and People" cards
Creation and promise	(Adam to Abraham; Gen. 1–11)
Patriarchs	(Abraham to Joseph; Gen. 12–50)
Slavery in Egypt	(400 years, Moses; Exodus 1–14)
Circling in the desert	(Moses to Joshua; Exodus 15–Deut. 34)
Conquering the land	(Joshua 1–24)
The time of judges	(Judges–Ruth 4)
We want a king!	(120 years; Saul, David, Solomon)
Divided kingdom	(1 Kings 12–25)
Exiled in Babylon	(70 years; 2 Kings 25–2 Chron. 36)
Returning to rebuild the Temple	(Zerubbabel, Ezra, Nehemiah; Ezra–Esther)
Jesus proclaimed Messiah	(Acts and New Testament Epistles)
Among the nations: forced to live in ghettos	(The Middle Ages and beyond)
British leave Palestine; a new state of Israel	(The year 1948 C.E. [common era])

The Shema

The creed of Judaism, the Shema, is found in Deuteronomy 6:4. Every practicing Jew believes this statement and seeks to do what follows in verse 5: "Love the LORD your God with all your heart and with all your soul and with all your strength."

It may help to read the Shema in various English translations:

- Hear, O Israel: The LORD our God, the LORD is one. (NIV)
- Hear, O Israel: The LORD our God is one LORD. (KJV)
- Hear, O Israel: The LORD is our God, the LORD alone. (NRSV)
- Hear, O Israel! The LORD is our God, the LORD is one! (NASB)
- O Israel, listen: Jehovah is our God, Jehovah alone. (LB)
- Hear, O Israel, the LORD is our God, one Lord. (NEB)

Service for Shabbat

In Real Life
Exploring tough questions facing youth today

Jews keep the Sabbath from sundown on Friday to sundown on Saturday every week, beginning and ending with Sabbath prayers. Here are the prayers and actions that take place just before the Friday evening meal is served, a way to respectfully observe the beginning of the Jewish Sabbath, or Shabbat.

With your group, decide if you will try the Anglicized Hebrew words (the English that follows them is the translation), or skip them.

(Light candles.)

We kindle the lights of shabbat, seeing them as symbols of human enlightenment and human kindness. Let us remember the generations before us who lit candles as we do, and found beauty and serenity in their light. Together we kindle the lights of shabbat.

Na-eh ha-or ba-olam. Na-eh ha-or ba-shalom. Na-eh ha-or ba-shabbat.

How wonderful is the light of the world. How radiant are the candles of peace. How beautiful are the lights of shabbat.

(Serve the wine substitute.)

Wine is the symbol of the wholeness of life. There are times when we drink from bitter cups, yet there are also times when we savor the sweetness and joy that exult life. Wine thus points to the recognition that life is both joy and sorrow. We re-solve to accept them both and so affirm all of life. These provide the happiness of which this cup speaks. Let us raise our cups to the fullness that is life.

Na-eh shalom ba-olam. Na-eh shalom ba-adam. Na-eh shalom ba-shabbat.

How wonderful is peace in the world. How glorious is peace among all people. How beautiful is the peace of shabbat.

(All present drink.)

SONG : *Hee-nay ma-tov u-ma-na-eem She-vet a-kheem gam ya-khad.*
Behold how good it is when brothers and sisters dwell together in unity.

(Serve the challah.)

As the fingers of the challah intertwine, so do we join hands in our common humanity, sharing the fruits of our labor. We cherish all that has been created through human effort. We celebrate the accomplishments of yesterday and today, anticipating the possibilities of tomorrow. May the sharing of this challah strengthen our bonds with others who walk upon this earth.

Na-eh a-mal ka-pay-noo. Na-eh le-khem ha-aretz. Na-eem ha-mo-tsee-eem le-khem meen ha-a-rets.

How beautiful is the work of our hands. How wonderful is the bread of the earth. How glorious are those who bring forth bread from the earth.

(All present eat challah.)

We honor the shabbat, a day of rest and peace. Throughout Jewish history, the observance of shabbat has served as a manifestation of human dignity. Shabbat is a gift we give ourselves—a gift of time to use as we wish. Let us celebrate together the end of another week in the company of friends and family.

SONG: *Shalom kha-vay-reem, shalom kha-vay-reem, Shalom, shalom!*
L'-heet ra-ot, l'-heet ra-ot, Shalom, shalom!

Peace to our friends
Until we meet again.
Peace.
Shabbat shalom!

Mantras, Menorahs, and Minarets : Session 4

Permission is granted to photocopy this handout for use with this session.

>>> **SESSION 5**

ISLAM—IS DOUBTING FOR BELIEVERS?

Exploring tough questions facing youth today

>>> KEY VERSE

Immediately the father of the child cried out, "I believe; help my unbelief!" (Mark 9:24)

>>> FAITH STORY

Mark 9:14-24

>>> FAITH FOCUS

When Jesus confronted the disciples with "you faithless generation" (v. 19), he was emphasizing the critical role of faith in confronting evil in the world. Yet even a man who struggled with faith was granted the healing of his son. Struggling with doubt can deepen our faith.

For Muslims, perhaps the most important religious concept is obedience to the guidance of Allah. Mohammed, the last of the prophets, established his example and the tradition of the community as a guiding light. True faith offers a series of specific directions for life. Thus, in any situation there will be no doubt about what to do.

>>> SESSION GOAL

Help participants explore different ways to deal with the intersection of faith and doubt.

TEACHING PLAN

>>> Materials needed and advance preparation

- Place two sheets of paper on opposite ends of the room, one with "I BELIEVE IT" written on it and the other with "I DOUBT IT" (for Focus)

- Copies of the handout sheet for Session 5

- Pieces of candy or other small prize for activity (Explore, *Option A*)

- Prepare five rolled-up pieces of newsprint with scrambled Pillar-statements on them (Explore, *Option A*)

- A bottle of drinking water prepared in advance with either plain water or mixed with salt (Apply, *Option A*)

- Index cards and pencils (Apply, *Option A*)

- Prayer mats, for ritual prayer (Apply, *Option B*)

- Chalkboard/chalk or newsprint/markers

1. FOCUS 5-7 minutes

I believe it/I doubt it. Post two sheets of paper on opposite ends of the room, one with "I BELIEVE IT" and the other with "I DOUBT IT." Tell the group you will be reading ten statements about faith. After each one, they must respond by quickly moving to the appropriate side of the room.

Use statements like these:

- God exists.
- Adam and Eve were real people.
- We know what Jesus looked like.
- There is absolute proof that Jesus rose from the dead.

In Real Life | Mantras, Menorahs, and Minarets   37

"In certain periods of history, the Christian church valued... pure assent, almost blind acceptance. 'I believe what the church believes' was a thoroughly acceptable personal testimony. Accept the church's teachings and you are a believer.

Now there is almost the opposite approach. 'No one is going to tell me what to believe. It's a personal matter, depending on how each person feels, depending on personal opinion.' [But] almost everyone appeals to some kind of authority upon which they base their deepest beliefs."

Gary Wilde,
The Quiet Hour

- We know who wrote each book of the Bible.
- We know what Jesus taught, through the things he wrote. (A sneaky one.)
- The rules for living are clear to all believers.
- All religions say basically the same things.
- Submitting to God is a one-time decision for a whole lifetime.
- Real faith means having no doubts.

Option: Supplement this opening with specific comparisons and contrasts between Islamic and Christian beliefs— and use an active response to help participants see what they may already know about Islam. Just add the exercise below as a "Part Two" in this step.

Again, read a series of statements, but this time instruct people to **stand up** (if they believe the statement is a truth held by **Christians** but not Muslims); or *bow down* (if they think it is a statement held by *Muslims* but not Christians). Clasp hands together if they think the statement is a truth held in common by both religions:

1. True religion began with Adam.
2. Fasting helps a person's spiritual growth.
3. Jesus was a great prophet.
4. Holy writings are only "the Word of God" when they are read in their original language.
5. Jesus died on a cross.
6. Abraham pointed the way toward God.
7. A true religion will seek political control of a nation.
8. The concept of a Trinity denies that there is only one God.
9. It's okay to eat pork.

Afterward, go back and explain the correct responses, elaborating as needed. Point out that numbers 1, 2, 3, and 6 are actually held in common by most Muslims and Christians. Statements 5 and
9 are Christian only. Statements 4, 7, and 8 are Muslim only.

2. CONNECT 10 minutes

Now invite stories about personal experiences with faith and doubt. Ask:

- *To what extent is your faith based on absolute certainty?*
- *When have you had significant doubts? What did you do about that?*
- *If you have doubts, does that mean you are not a good believer? Why, or why not?*

3. EXPLORE THE STORIES 18-20 minutes

Shift to this activity by saying: *The word "Islam" means "surrender" or "submit to God." For Muslims, submitting to God requires accepting everything in the Qur'an (Koran)—with absolute certainty and proclaiming it with complete dedication. Is it the same for Christians? What, in a practical sense, does "complete surrender to the will of God" mean? Let's look into it....*

Help your group get a feel for Islam, especially its historical development and the emphasis on surrender to God. Deal with the two stories—of Islam and Christianity—in turn.

The Story of Islam

⟫ **Option A:** Distribute copies of the handout sheet. Give participants a chance to read through the story of Mohammed silently. When everyone is through reading, inform the group that you will retell the story in your own words *but you will insert 3 incorrect facts.* They are to listen closely to catch these wrong facts:

Incorrect Statement #1: Instead of "the Angel Gabriel" say: "Michael the Archangel."
Incorrect Statement #2: Instead of "Medina" say: "Kartoum."
Incorrect Statement #3: Instead of "Judas" say: "Joseph of Arimathea."

Participants must turn over their handout sheets so they can't follow word for word. (There's a prize involved!) They should stand up immediately (silently) when they catch one of the incorrect facts. If they are correct, award a small prize (such as a piece of candy). If the "catch" is in error, they are out of the competition.

Now summarize: *As Mohammed went on to spread his power politically, the Qur'an became a rule of life. Muslims believe that Allah has not made it too hard to be good and faithful—unlike Christianity, whose standard is seen as impossible (for example, the Bible says: "Be perfect"). But Allah has prescribed Five Pillars of the Faith, actions anyone can carry out. If these are done out of heartfelt dedication, one is acceptable to God and a true Muslim.*

⟫ **What Are The Five Pillars?**
In advance, prepare five pieces of newsprint with scrambled Pillar-statements on them, as shown below in bold. Post them on the wall after designating teams to see which one can unscramble all the words first.

Pillar #1: Blipcu Yitonmets. (Public Testimony; Leader's explanation: A person becomes a Muslim by reciting the *shahadah* before others, namely: "There is no God but Allah, and Mohammed is his messenger." The faithful utter this statement as often as possible every day.)

Pillar #2: Liday Turali Raryeps. (Daily Ritual Prayers; Leader's explanation: Muslims practice a ritual of prayer five times daily, bowing in the direction of the holy city, Mecca. They pray at dawn, midday, mid-afternoon, sundown, and nightfall. Strong-voiced prayer-heralds, the *muezzin*, call the community to prayer from the towers of the mosque, or recordings ring out over loudspeakers.)

Pillar #3: Vingig Mals ot het Ropo. (Giving Alms to the Poor; Leader's explanation: Originally Islam preached voluntary, charitable giving to the poor. Now, in Muslim countries, almsgiving is assessed as a tax at 2-10% of one's wealth. It is considered a loan given to Allah, which will be repaid in the afterlife.)

Pillar #4: Gatsfni rof a Mhotn. (Fasting for a Month; Leader's explanation: During the ninth month of the Muslim lunar year, Ramadan, the faithful are required to fast during daylight hours. They abstain from all food, drink, smoking, and sex. After nightfall, however, the feasting begins. The Ramadan fast is a commemoration of the month in which Mohammed first received his revelations from Allah.)

Pillar #5: Egliprami ot Cemca. (Pilgrimage to Mecca; Leader's explanation: Called the *hajj*, this visit is required at least once in a lifetime. Pilgrims dress in simple white tunics and sandals, so that rich and poor cannot be distinguished. They walk from the outskirts of Mecca to the Kabbah and make seven trips around it before kissing the sacred black stone. On the tenth day of the pilgrimage they may sacrifice a sheep or goat.)

Today, there are about 1.8 billion Muslims, or 24% of the world's population, making Islam the second-largest religion.

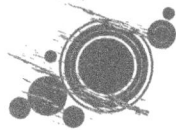

What about the 72 virgins?
You may have heard about the popular tradition that Paradise is a pleasant oasis where a man's every desire is satisfied either by his wife or by beautiful *houris*, or virgins. If this question arises, put those who are interested on an online search for the real back-story, or have them inquire with a local *imam* (Muslim cleric) or scholar; have them compare findings.

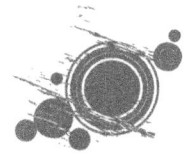

"Islam" means "surrender"; Muslims are ones who have submitted their whole life to the will of Allah.

Note:

If you are doing the Extender Session, finalize your plans now.

When each of the Pillars has been successfully unscrambled, and a winning team declared, go back and explain each with the "Leader's explanation," above, as well as the Insights section and your own additional reading.

>> **Option:** If you have time, further discuss any of the Pillars by asking:

- *How would this be a good thing to do—for anyone? How could it help your spiritual growth?*

>> **Option B:** Use one or more of these YouTube videos for the introduction to Islam:

- https://youtu.be/Nw4jjOr-4gY (4 min.) Raises awareness of the real facets of Islam which could be appreciated by non-Muslims from all quarters of the world.
- https://youtu.be/eKB50GYMQ9g (10 min.) John Green (fast-paced & fun!)

Wrap up this option by pointing out that Islam and Christianity are concerned about many of the same things—the oneness and sovereignty of God, revelation and mercy, human responsibility, the afterlife, and the divine call to obedience.

The Christian Story

Now bring in the Bible story. Read Mark 9:14-24 aloud and ask:

- *In light of what you now understand of the Muslim emphasis on surrender, commitment, and submission, how do you think a Muslim might view the father's personal testimony in verse 24?* (Possible response: He won't get his child healed because he doesn't have enough faith. To question is to be weak.)
- *How well does verse 24 work for you, as a personal statement of faith? Why?*

4. APPLY 6 minutes

Focus attention back on the Bible story for a moment. Comment: *From the father's perspective, Jesus might or might not be able to help the son in a miraculous way. The father had some doubt; he said: "If you are able." Both Muslims and Christians say, "Believe, and witness to your belief." Yet here is a Bible story about someone who believed AND doubted. That was apparently okay!*

>> **Option A:** Place your prepared bottle of drinking water in front of the group and explain that it is either pure water or has been salted. Ask:

- *How tough would it be to "swallow your doubts" about this water?* (Let someone try the water!)
- *How "tough to swallow" are all the things you've been taught in the church in your life so far?*

After fielding some general responses, distribute index cards and invite participants to write specific doubts they have now, have had in the past, or think they might have in the future. Explain that these can involve anything about their faith that they have been taught. Ask them to jot as many of these doubts—large or small—on the cards, one per card, and throw them into a pile. Shuffle the cards and read them aloud to the group, one at a time, without comment.

>> **Option B: Ritual experience. Daily Prayer.** Invite a Muslim leader from a local Mosque to teach the group how to practice the daily ritual prayer. For specific instructions, one of these websites may be helpful:

- http://www.al-islam.org/articles/laws-practices-how-perform-daily-prayers
- http://www.icsconline.org/docs/MuslimPrayerbyJihadTurkandJoshHerman.pdf

A version of the *surat fatiha* prayer can be found here: https://youtu.be/xCwtpNgFw5g. Here is an English translation of the words of the prayer:

> In the name of God,
> Most Gracious,
> Most Merciful;
> Praise be to God,
>   the cherisher and Sustainer of the worlds;
> Most Gracious, Most Merciful;
> Master of the Day of Judgment.
> Thee do we worship,
>   and Thine aid we seek.
> Show us the straight way,
>   the Way of those on whom Thou has bestowed Thy goodness,
>   those whose portion is not wrath,
>   and who go not astray.

5. RESPOND 10 minutes

Begin this step by saying: *There is value in doubt if we let it push us to seek out answers.*

Ask participants to pick one doubt or "big question" they have. (Perhaps it was one of the doubts shared in Connect or Apply, Option A.) Ask: *What will help you seek the answers?*

Brainstorm specific plans and information sources. Work together to develop a "Doubt Exploration Plan." Include in the plan (write on chalkboard or newsprint):

- The question(s) I hope to answer.
- The people or sources I could consult.
- The times and dates I will give to this search.
- The date I will report my findings.

Close with these thoughts: *For Muslims, belief means having absolute certainty, and acting on it. The Bible, on the other hand, includes stories of those who had doubts, and allows for doubts as part of the process of maturing and growing in faith.*

INSIGHTS FROM HOLY WRITINGS

>> THE FINAL MESSAGE ENCOUNTERS A GROWING FAITH

Philip Hitti, in *Basic Beliefs*, says: "Islam is a totalitarian religion in the sense that it strives to regulate every aspect of the life of the believer, holding no clear-cut distinction between what is secular and what is spiritual."

Yet the *Qur'an* (also spelled Koran) clearly distinguishes between those who believe and those who don't. For Muslims, belief is much less an inner attitude or state of mind than an action to be carried out in daily prayer and a lifetime commitment to the other four pillars of faith. To state the *shahada* before Muslim witnesses is to gain entrance into the *ummah*, the community of true believers, and live for Allah's will in the world.

> "The Church regards with esteem also the Muslims. They adore the one God... merciful and all-powerful, the Creator of heaven and earth... They revere [Jesus] as a prophet. They also honor Mary, His virgin Mother... [T]hey value the moral life and worship God especially through prayer, almsgiving, and fasting."
>
> *Declaration on the Relation of the Church to Non-Christian Religions*, 3.

> **Christian belief is acceptance coupled with understanding, trust paired with the exploration of doubts, peaceful dependence joined with a commitment to action.**

> **"Moreover, we resolutely declare that religions must never incite war, hateful attitudes, hostility and extremism, nor must they incite violence or the shedding of blood. These tragic realities are the consequence of a deviation from religious teachings"**
>
> Pope Francis and Ahmad Al-Tayyeb, *A Document on Human Fraternity for World Peace and Living Together*, 4 February 2019

From its beginning, Islam did not deny the validity of other religions, but viewed itself as the com-pletion of what had begun in the other religions. Muslims do point to the errors of Jews in waiting for Elijah and of Christians in assenting to the "three gods" of the Trinity. On the other hand, Muslims recognize Jews and Christians as fellow "people of the book." Muslims also consider Jesus a great prophet who preached many marvelous and truthful sermons, and that he will come again before the last judgment. But Islam sees neither Jesus nor Mohammed as divine; there is only one God. Mohammed received God's word, and this one man's message corrects the skewed beliefs of all other religions. Mohammed was God's final messenger.

Mohammed went to Medina to increase his popular support and political power, and in order to spread his message about the one true God—Allah. Here again is a contrast with the Way of Jesus, who modeled the way of suffering love, and was willing to be misunderstood and mistreated in order to highlight God's redemptive power of love. Jesus preached an "upside down" kingdom; Islam equates success of ventures as a sign of Allah's approval.

Thus, in Christian spirituality, faith cannot demand that the outcome of the journey be crystal clear at its beginning. For Christians, faith always has a quality of hope, even when that hope is not yet clearly seen.

No doubt this was the attitude of the father in Mark 24. Surely his eyes were on his son when he uttered these words, though the words were directed to Jesus. According to the biblical account, the man soon saw something quite marvelous!

» WISDOM FOR TODAY...

Which takes more faith in God? To be assured victory if righteous, or to be promised only the redemptive effects of potential failure? Most young people today expect to get exactly what they pay for. The gospel, in contrast to Islam, offers no such guarantee. After all, we sometimes—surprisingly—receive much more than we ever expected.

The Angel Speaks!

Exploring tough questions facing youth today

In the Arabian desert, around 600 years after Jesus, a young caravan leader with an intense yearning for God began going up into the hills to pray and meditate. What happened to him on one particular "Night of Power," when he was about 40 years old, would change the course of history. That night was the beginning of a new faith that would eventually claim more than a billion and a half followers worldwide.

> On that apparently miraculous night, an angel came to Mohammed and said:
> *Proclaim!*
> *In the name of thy Lord and Cherisher*
> *Who created—*
> > *Created man out of a mere clot*
> > > *of congealed blood.*

The angel (later identified as the Angel Gabriel) continued giving messages direct from Allah over the next several years. Since Mohammed was completely illiterate, he had to memorize the messages until others could write them down. Eventually all the messages were gathered into one book, the *Qur'an* (also spelled Koran), the holy book of the Muslim faith.

Though he was at first terrified, these experiences of revelation changed Mohammed for good. He had been concerned for years about the spiritual lives of his people. The clans warred with each other, each one claiming allegiance to various gods. This distressed the young man, because the message he received from God was very clear: There is only one God, Allah, who must be obeyed without question. This was the message that Mohammed began to preach powerfully in his hometown of Mecca. ("Islam" means "surrender"; Muslims are ones who have submitted their whole life to the will of Allah.)

Most of the citizens of Mecca, who considered themselves a religious people long before Mohammed, scorned this young evangelist and his message. They worshiped at the Kabbah, originally a shrine supposedly built by Abraham, which housed a shiny black stone (a meteorite from ancient times), honored as sacred. Also in the building were various statues of other deities, which the clans came to worship each year. Such polytheism (the worship of many gods) was abhorrent to Mohammed with his revealed message of the one God. Yet the tribe overseeing the Kabbah made lots of money from the tourist trade of yearly pilgrims. The tribe and Mohammed became enemies.

Though opposition to the young prophet grew, he did make some converts in Mecca. Yet when his life was repeatedly threatened, he fled his hometown. Six leaders from Medina, 200 miles to the north, came to invite Mohammed to be their political and social leader. They had heard of his leadership and wisdom. So Mohammed left for his new home in 622 C.E. This event is known as the *hijra (hegira)*, "the flight." It is the official beginning of the Islamic era.

From Medina, Mohammed built his political and military power. Eventually he returned to Mecca in 630 C.E., with an army of 10,000, to claim the city for Islam. He continued to preach allegiance to the one God. He taught that the Jews and Christians had benefited from many true prophets in the past (such as Abraham, Moses, Elijah, and Jesus). But their holy books had been corrupted and needed reforming (for example, it only *appeared* that Jesus had been crucified; according to Islam, it was actually Judas who was rightly punished on the cross). The revelations to Mohammed, the final and greatest prophet, were God's final message to all peoples.

Mantras, Menorahs, and Minarets : Session 5

Permission is granted to photocopy this handout for use with this session.

>>> EXTENDER SESSION
(best used after Session 5)

QUESTION AND ANSWER

>> **Option A:** More Questions to Answer

Session goal: Follow up on questions generated in Session 1 and throughout the study.

Plan: Spend time doing a "Questions to Answer" review, based on the Apply activity in Session 1. Study the poster you hung on the wall with questions participants wanted to answer. Spend a session discussing the questions that have not yet been answered. Be sure that you, as leader, go through them in advance in order to develop your own basic response, and gather other resources to help you supplement your responses. You might also be prepared to suggest scripture passages that relate to the questions and potential answers.

>> **Option B:** Worship with Another Faith

Session goal: Experience the worship of another faith.

Plan: Plan to visit the worship service or site (temple, community center, etc.) of another religion. Or invite a group presentation by a leader of another faith introducing that religion. Prepare for this visit by developing a series of questions to ask, such as the ones on page 6 of Session 1 of this course.

In Real Life
Exploring tough questions facing youth today

CLUELESS AND CALLED
Discipleship and the Gospel of Mark

What does it take to be a disciple? This study of the Gospel of Mark focuses on the requirements for following Jesus' way and the abundant life that is ours as a result. (5 sessions)

DO MIRACLES HAPPEN?
Signs and Wonders in the Gospel of John

The greatest miracle, recorded in John 1:14 and 3:16, is the miracle of God's love that became flesh and lived among us. But John also included examples of what we more traditionally think of as miracles: the wonder of abundance from little; healing; signs of impossibility and faith; and the resurrection. (5 sessions)

DO THE RIGHT THING
Ethics Shaped by Faith

How do you know what's right and what's wrong? Even when you figure it out, the right thing is often the unpopular or unpleasant choice. This unit offers participants a clearer sense of what it means to claim a faith identity, a foundation that can help them sort out the gritty details of ethics shaped by faith. (6 sessions)

FIGHT RIGHT
A Christian Approach to Conflict Resolution

This unit will help youth understand conflict and its function. They will learn how they can be honest and loving, and explore how conflict can be used for positive results. They will also learn ways to enhance their communication skills. 1 Corinthians. (5 sessions)

GOD IS A WARRIOR?
Violence in the Bible

The Bible challenges us to be reconciled to one another and work for justice. So what do we do with the stories that seem to condone violence or even encourage it? A discussion of issues in the Old and New Testaments. (6 sessions)

HOW DO YOU KNOW?
Wisdom in the Bible

Wisdom literature teaches us that we gain knowledge of the world, ourselves, and God through experience and observation. This unit provides practical, hands-on wisdom to help young people avoid life's snares and grow closer to God. Proverbs, Job, Ecclesiastes. (5 sessions)

HOW TO BE A TRUE FRIEND
The Bible Reveals Friendship's Heart

To be a friend takes skill. Help youth discover the secrets of friendship through various stories from the Old and New Testament. (6 sessions)

HOW TO READ THE BIBLE
Building Skills for Bible Study

What kind of book is the Bible? What does this book mean to me? This unit looks at the Bible as revelation, as history, as literature. Selected scripture. (5 sessions)

KEEPING THE GARDEN
A Faith Response to God's Creation

If Christians believe that God made the world, we do not need any more compelling reason to care for it than that God has handed us a treasure to hold and protect. This unit gets beyond trendy environmentalism and challenges youth to see environmental awareness as a religious issue. Genesis. (6 sessions)

MANTRAS, MENORAHS, AND MINARETS
Encountering Other Faiths

How is Christianity different from other faiths? Why do others believe the way they do? This study can give youth a new appreciation for the uniqueness of Jesus. Selected scripture. (5 sessions)

SALT, LIGHT, AND THE GOOD LIFE
The Beatitudes and the Sermon on the Mount

What can youth expect in a life of discipleship? This unit explores the Sermon on the Mount under four main sections: the Beatitudes, Salt and Light, Jesus and the Law, and Heavenly Teachings. Matthew 5. (6 sessions)

A SPECK IN THE UNIVERSE
The Bible on Self-Esteem and Peer Pressure

Discover God's unconditional love and acceptance of all people. This study will show positive ways to have one's life make a difference, and help youth find ways to resist negative peer pressure and turn it into positive action. (6 sessions)

THE RADICAL REIGN
Parables of Jesus

Jesus used parables to reveal what the kingdom of God is like, and how God relates to us. This study highlights how the parables reveal God's reign as radically different from the world we live in, and what that means for the Christian life. (6 sessions)

TESTING THE WATERS
Basic Tenets of Faith

Discover the biblical roots for the central Christian concepts of covenant, community, and baptism. This short course is a way to test the (baptismal) waters of Christianity before diving in, or review the basics for those who already have. (6 sessions)

WHO IS GOD?
Engaging the Mystery

God is beyond human comprehension, yet desires to be known. These sessions focus on the way we get clues about and glimpses of God from the Bible, God's creation, and church tradition. Selected scripture. (5 sessions)

www.ingramcontent.com/pod-product-compliance
Lightning Source LLC
Chambersburg PA
CBHW080408170426
43193CB00016B/2856